INDOMITABLE

HOW I SPENT 37 YEARS IN WISCONSIN PRISONS AND CAME OUT BETTER THAN I WENT IN

BY

HARLAN RICHARDS

ISBN 979-8-9932788-0-3
Copyright 2025
Copper Falls Publishing
Marshfield, Wisconsin

WHAT PRISON TEACHES

I don't trust anybody
Who is nice to me.
People aren't nice
Unless they want
Something from you that
You don't want to give them.
The most adept predators
Know that
Velvet glove over steel fist
Often gets the best result.

Harlan Richards
August 22, 2011

CONTENTS

DEDICATION

This book is dedicated to the Holy Spirit who resides within me always, directs my steps and guides me through the pitfalls of life. I pray that the Holy Spirit will guide my hand to make this work an inspirational discourse which will empower and enlighten others.

ACKNOWLEDGEMENT

Iowe a debt of gratitude to Cay Villars for the changes she wrought in my life. As always, once I think I know everything worth knowing, someone comes along to demonstrate to me that I have a long way yet to go on the path toward illumination.

INTRODUCTION

I once read a book by Pat Croce called "I Feel Great." His theory or philosophy on life is that you are free to choose the way you feel. Whenever someone asked me how I was doing I always said "Fantastic!", which often caused a reaction from the listener because I was serving a life sentence in prison during the height of the Mass Incarceration Movement. But I came to learn that what you choose becomes a self-fulfilling prophesy and the more I told others I was fantastic, the more fantastic I became.

Anyway, I reached the point in my life where I was a walking, talking aphorism. I crammed so many pithy sayings into my head and my heart that they seemed to spill back out on a regular basis. I was speaking to my roommates one night while still in prison and was told I should write a book to which I replied that I wouldn't know what to call it. That is when they coined the term "Harlanisms". As I was considering writing a book for several years, I decided that having a unique title was as good a reason to start as any. But time changes all things and what I once thought would be a good title for a memoir turned into a title for a much different book. It was only after the ordeal of 37 years in prison (and many further changes within me) that the current title revealed itself. This is an abridged version of my life story which I started writing in prison and am finally finishing more than 3 years after my release.

DISCLAIMER

This is a memoir, not an autobiography. I have omitted many of the examples of my conduct which occurred before I was sent to prison for murder. It is not my intent to create a dry recitation of the unfolding of my life. Rather, I seek to show in general terms what sort of person I was before I gave my life to God and what sort of person I am now. Most of the time I omitted the names of the people involved in my escapades because I do not want to hurt anybody or to bring unwanted attention to other people who would probably not want their involvement in those incidents made public.

Rest assured, however, that every factual assertion in this book is true and accurate to the best of my knowledge, belief and memory. If I inadvertently made any incorrect statement of fact I apologize and will promptly make any necessary corrections if and when they are brought to my attention.

PROLOGUE

I hear birds singing. Not real birds. Electronic birds. It is my alarm clock telling me it is 4:15 a.m. and time to get up and go to work. I have to hurry because breakfast is served at 4:30 a.m. I get up, get dressed and head to the bathroom to wash up. Usually, my timing is good and I can get to an open sink right away. I have just enough time to do everything I need to do and make it to breakfast on time.

It is the start of another day. At 5:30 A.M., I will leave with the rest of the guys on work release to go pack beef jerky all day long. It is not hard work. Boring, tedious and unpleasant? Yes. But hard? Not really. Except for me. I have a crippled leg from a motorcycle accident as a teen which causes me pain from standing and walking on concrete in a refrigerated building all day long. It is the price I must pay at this point in my life. You see I am serving a life sentence in prison for killing a man many years ago. If I want to earn a parole, I must be on work release. The only work release job available to me at Gordon Correctional Center is at Jack Link's beef jerky factory. So, pain or no pain, I'm off to another day of work.

How did I end up like this? How could I have made so many bad decisions in my life to put me here? Well, it all began many years ago ...

I GROW UP

I was born January 17, 1954 to a Sicilian-American mother and a mixed-ethnicity white father. I guess he could be called the quintessential melting-pot-American because he has so many different strains of European immigrants as ancestors. The first of his forebears came over on the Mayflower. I found that out because my father told me that we were part Native American and I wanted to find out the tribe from which I descended. When I did the research, I found out that there was nary a Native in the family tree but there was a rich history of diverse immigrants. The "Richards" name that I carry is an Anglicized German name from an immigrant who came over in the 1850s. My mother's father came over from Sicily in 1900 at age 17. It must have been quite an adventure for him at that age.

I don't remember my birth. I was told it was a cold winter night. Nor do I remember my older brother grabbing me by the feet as I lay on the couch and dumping me on the floor my first day home from the hospital. And I can't remember the time he tried to stick a scissors down my throat or a screwdriver up my ass. It was what I was told while growing up and recorded by my mother in my baby book. The subsequent experiences I do

1

remember lead me to believe it is all true. I barely remember being a sickly baby and having to go to the hospital for an ordeal of some sort. I was allergic to cow's milk and in the 1950s many mothers were told not to breastfeed their babies. The end result was that I was given a soy substitute which so irritated my bowels that I required some sort of rectal surgery as a toddler. My very survival was in doubt. From there I grew into a sickly, weak child. I remember my father calling me into the kitchen on evenings when I was just a toddler and making me drink warm milk which begs the question: How could I be allergic to cow's milk as a baby and a few years later be given warm cow's milk to help fatten me up? It makes no sense to me.

Looking back on it all, I can say I was born into a love-starved home where I was abused and victimized for years. But at the time I was living it I didn't have a clue that anything was amiss. It was just the way things were. Since I had never experienced anything else I had no other situation to compare it to.

I was fortunate in many ways. My parents loved me. They both worked very hard to earn enough money to provide their two children with a comfortable middle-class life with all the benefits of growing up in America. They both came from large families and grew up surrounded with love and support from their siblings. They did not recognize the need to provide their children with love and affection and hugs and kisses. They had experienced much more abusive childhoods than I had, yet they weathered them well and I think this was due to the support of their siblings. In retrospect, I can see that my brother's intense hatred of me and desire to hurt me was based on his own unfulfilled need for love. There was so little affection in his little family that when I came along and took up the immediate attention of our parents he was left alone and ignored. Hence, the jealousy and attacks against me.

When people used to ask me as a child what I wanted to be when I grew up, I always said the same thing: a dumbbell, because then I wouldn't have to go to school. My plan didn't work out and I was sent to kindergarten at the appointed time. Everything started out ok. I liked all the little girls and I thought it great fun to run around kissing them. Apparently, they didn't see it the same way I did and told their parents who complained to my parents who made me stop. I had never been around girls my age so I didn't know I wasn't supposed to kiss them. I had no idea how I was supposed to interact with the other kids. Nobody told me and I couldn't figure it out for myself. After that, I was afraid to interact with anyone and kept pretty much to myself.

For a while my grandmother (my father's mother) stayed with us and took care of my brother Russell and me while our parents were at work. During the summer, I would wait until her back was turned and take off on my bike. I must have been only about 4 years old and still had training wheels on my bike. But I knew she wouldn't come looking for me and I pretty much ran wild in the neighborhood for hours. She would always tell my father who would yell at me but pretty soon I would be back at it again. I really can't remember what I used to do on these excursions but I remember taking them and the feeling of freedom I had when I did so.

My other grandmother, the Sicilian one, also took care of us when we were little. Our mother would drop us off at our grandmother's house in downtown Madison on her way to work and we would spend the day. I really didn't like it there. My grandfather could barely speak English and my father would not let us learn Italian. He scared me and I could not understand him when he talked to me. I remember being in the basement (where my grandparents lived most of the time) and hearing him screaming upstairs while the doctor cut off his toes that had become infected because of his diabetes. He died when I was 5 years old. My mother and her sisters always talked about diabetes being an inherited disease but that it skipped generations so they wouldn't have to worry about it. Ignorance is bliss. Their generation never exercised and ate whatever they wanted. All of them ended up with diabetes and heart disease caused by lack of exercise, poor diet and hereditary factors. I remember seeing the name of my grandmother's sister, Santina, on a list of phone numbers posted by her phone. The name stuck with me and when I grew up, I named my daughter Santina. I don't think she appreciated the name I gave her as she goes by Tina these days.

I was skinny as a rail when I started school but after a few years, I blew up like a balloon. I started eating everything in sight. My parents, impervious to such notions as fitness and nutrition, let me stuff myself to my heart's content. As a result, I became very fat and was disliked by just about everyone in school. I quickly learned that the best way to get respect was by beating up the other kids.

I was no stranger to beatings as my brother routinely beat up on me. My parents never did, though. And for that I am very grateful. Russell was crafty and sly and knew how to inflict pain and suffering on me outside of the presence of any adults. He was just as good at emotional pain as he was at physical pain. It was so bad my parents told me to throw my toys at him to defend myself when I was little. But I was really too intimidated by him to fight back much at all and suffered in silence. There was one time when he and I were waiting for our mother in her car outside of my Aunt Jane's house that I threw caution to the wind. I slammed his hand in the car door and while it was stuck, I beat him up. I thought my mother would be proud of me but she was very angry and I got punished instead. I couldn't figure that out. Punished for finally standing up for myself? It left me confused and all the more at his mercy because I was afraid to fight back for fear of being punished. I was such a love-starved kid that I wanted affection and attention more than anything else but rarely ever got it.

As the years went by in grade school, I became more aggressive and bullying. I always excelled in school work. It was easy for me, too easy, as I was usually done way ahead of everybody else and sat there bored waiting for the others to catch up. I probably should have been in an advanced class of some sort but there was no such thing around back then. I was always getting teased by the other kids which would make me mad and I would beat up my tormentors and get into trouble. I also had a bed wetting problem, no doubt a symptom of my emotional problems. At the time, all I knew was that I went to bed dry and woke up wet. This lasted until I was 12 and was quite an inconvenience.

Out of school, Russell was still my primary companion. As I said before, since I never knew any other life than the one I was living, the way he treated me was just the way it was and I had no idea I was being mistreated. It was only how I turned out later and tracing it back to its causes that gave me the insight I needed to change. Or maybe that is just how I was and I'm using him to justify my basic evil nature? Hmm? Food for thought. Maybe all those times I cried myself to sleep were just a normal part of growing up. Maybe my inferiority complex, lack of self-esteem, insecurity, self-hatred and loneliness were part of my basic nature and had nothing to do with how I was treated. Well, it is what it is and I'll let you draw your own conclusions.

As a child, I lived in a wonderful house. It was a sizeable 2-storey house on a quiet residential street on the West side of Madison. There was a fairly large wooded area across the street several hundred yards wide and perhaps a mile long. It had a drainage ditch running through it and it was shaped like a large valley. No paving, just the natural drainage path of the snow melt and storm runoff. We called it the creek. We climbed trees, made forts, cut spears, made bows and arrows, played games and enjoyed the variety and splendor of the woods.

When I first learned to walk, I wasn't very good at it. In fact, I was so bad I kept tripping over my own feet. My father, being the empathetic, loving man that he was, decided that I was doing it on purpose and resolved to break me of the habit by calling me Stumble Bum. He called me that for years and it didn't help improve my walking or running skills. I remember running down the sidewalk by my grandma's house and tripping over my feet and falling flat on my face. Not just once, every time I ran. I fell down and skinned my knees so much they got infected and I had to go to the hospital for a couple of days to get the infection under control. But it never stopped me from running and falling down.

Stumble-Bum

He laughed at me and called me Stumble-bum.
    Could I help it
        My feet had a mind of their own?
Later, he claimed, he thought
        I did it on purpose.
Even when my knees were
    Skinned so many times,
        I was hospitalized with infection.
Grown men should always taunt
    Four-year olds by calling them
        Stumble-bum when they fall down.
It was only after my kindergarten
    Teacher, seeing my problem, gave me
        Therapy to learn to use my legs,
That he pretended to be sorry
    For calling me Stumble-bum.
        I know better.
He called his four-year old son
    Stumble-bum because that's how
        Boys are made into men.

January 29, 2010

I took my unique ability to trip over my own two feet to kindergarten with me where I continued to fall flat on my face until the teachers gave me some simple coordination exercises to do. I ceased to trip and fall down any more. My father, upon being informed that I had a coordination problem that required therapy to fix, expressed remorse for calling me Stumble Bum for all those years. I didn't believe a word of it.

At the age of five or so I had my first BB gun. I can remember going down to the local grocery store to buy BBs for 5 cents per pack. I would load my gun and go off to the woods to hunt squirrels, rabbits and birds. I don't think that I ever hit anything I aimed at or ever managed to shoot an animal but it wasn't for lack of trying. I simply didn't know what I was doing and I made so much noise that any animal could hear me coming long before it saw me. The gray squirrels had a rough time though. We would chase them from tree to tree shooting at them. I guess we must have hit them a time or two because they sure scurried along every time we shot at them. The BB guns we had back then were not very powerful and the BBs couldn't do much more than sting a squirrel even if we would have managed to hit one. In fact, we used to put on a couple of sets of clothes and our swim masks and have shootouts with each other using BB guns.

Quite a few windows in my parents' house had those telltale little round holes where a BB hit. There was not enough force to shatter the window, just to punch a small hole. After I got older, I got a pellet gun but it didn't change my results. I still never bagged any game.

One time, I desperately wanted there to be a regular stream running through the woods so I found a spot and kneeled down and prayed with all my might that a miracle would occur and that a stream would bubble up at that spot. I prayed long and hard and that one thing I wanted so badly from God he never gave me. And I would not forgive him for abandoning me like that. It is the point where I lost my faith in Him as a child.

Our house was in an old neighborhood on the edge of Madison. There was a lot of expansion during the years I was growing up and constant construction going on not too far away. My brother and I would take our wagon to the construction sites and haul away scrap lumber by the pile. From this we would make tree forts and other things. We started making wooden go-carts with our scrap lumber that we could use to coast downhill. The front wheels were mounted on each end of a 2 by 4 which was attached to the cart with one bolt in the center which allowed it to swivel. We scrounged old tires from tricycles or wagons and hammered everything together with nails. We could rest our feet on the 2 by 4 and use our feet to steer or else tie a rope to each side of the 2 by 4 and pull the rope to steer. There wasn't that much steering to do anyway as all we ever did was coast down the hill which was pretty much a straight shot. Our brakes were a stick with some old rubber from a bicycle tire wrapped around it and nailed to the frame. To stop we pulled on one end of the stick which forced the rubber down on the pavement and slowed us down. Our house was on a bend in the road at the base of a fairly steep hill which was about one block to the top. The street went fairly level for the distance of two houses and then had a long, gradual decline for two blocks. We would push our carts up to the top of the hill and let 'er rip. Brakes were rarely used and mostly we just coasted down to the front of our house. The lower hill was much longer but slower going and not enough of a thrill to justify having to haul the go-cart back home.

I don't know how we ever learned to make this stuff. We just picked up the tools laying around the garage and started using them. My father had a pretty good assortment of hand tools. I don't remember ever seeing him use them very much. He also had a large assortment of nails, screws and misc. hardware. We cut, we hammered, we built. I don't recall ever having been shown how to do any of this. We just sorta figured it out as we went along.

My father was a tough guy, though not very big. He was about the size I have been for most of my adult life. He was 5'8" tall and about 150 pounds. But he loved to brawl as a young man and only quit when he was in his 30s and my mother threatened to leave him if he didn't stop getting into fights when they went out in the evenings. He taught me how to fight - actually he told me what fighting consisted of but never really taught me any sparring techniques. It was another one of those things he instilled in me at a very young age, early in grade school or before that. The lesson I took more to heart since I understood it better was that I was not allowed to lose no matter what. I must always win. Funny thing about that lesson. It is still with me today and has been the cause of a fair amount of difficulty in my life. Yet, on the other hand, I cannot imagine how I would have turned out had he not taught me that.

My father was emotionally distant. He did not give love and affection to anybody. He felt love, he just didn't share it. Hugs? Kind words? Encouragement? You gotta be kidding! He also liked to drink. Another habit I acquired by watching him. My parents used to have card games and occasional parties at their house and I was always allowed to drink, even as young as 5 years old. At that age, I could only take a sip of what they were drinking. I had no clue that alcohol had any effect on me until I was older. Around age 12 or so I began to appreciate the pleasure of getting drunk. After all, men are hard drinkers. The sooner I became a hard drinker, the sooner I became a man. My father smoked like a chimney and ultimately died of emphysema (later, I found out that it was a combination of silicosis and smoking which caused the emphysema). No surprise there. But in his day, no one but the tobacco companies knew that tobacco could kill you. When I was very young - 4 or 5 - I used to beg him for a cigarette so I could walk around with it in my mouth and pretend I was a smoker just like daddy.

In the 5th grade I learned about smoking for real and shoplifting. How else could a ten-year-old get cigarettes? Actually, we had lots of ways. For one, just look for a cigarette machine in a seldom-used lobby (such as in a theater, a bowling alley or gas station). Or find an older person to buy us a pack. But stealing worked best. My father bought his Winstons by the carton and threw them into his drawer in the kitchen where he kept all his papers and what-not that he didn't want to have to look for. He would throw the whole carton in there and reach in for a pack whenever he needed one. Since he smoked 2-3 packs a day it was easy to occasionally pilfer a pack without it being noticed. Of course it worked for alcohol, too. Just wait until the folks drank some and then take a little out of each bottle. Sometimes when I took a lot, I added in a bit of water to make up for it. But not too much or the liquor would taste weak and my father could detect that.

I learned which stores were the best for stealing cigarettes and I got one of my cousins started on it, too. We would go to the grocery store at Hilldale Shopping Center and take packs of cigarettes from a closed checkout line when no one was looking. The freezer for popsicles was nearby so I would toss a popsicle to my cousin standing near the counter and as he reached out to catch it near the cigarette rack he would grab a pack of smokes at the same time.

One time an older boy watched us and confronted us outside the store. I had the cigarettes so my cousin blocked him and told me to take off and get away. But as they fought, I realized that I couldn't leave him. He wasn't a fighter like I was and I couldn't bear the thought of deserting him while he got beat up. We had our bikes with us. We did most of our traveling at that age on bikes. I dropped my bike and went into the fray. There wasn't any fight after all. The guy thought he was going to bully us and when it didn't work, he settled for just talking to us.

We finally got caught because my brother told on me. My family went up north to a cottage for a week with some friends of my parents. They had several kids, two of which were the same ages as my brother and me. I wasted no time in indoctrinating my fellow playmate into the joys of stealing and smoking. I stole a cheap paring knife at a nearby store and my brother saw it. He tried to blackmail me and I wouldn't go along with it, mostly because I knew if I gave in it would never end. So he told on me about the knife and I broke under pressure and confessed everything else. My folks were pissed but I don't remember what the punishment was. I do remember that I was no longer allowed to hang out with my cousin.

A few years later, it was a different ball game with my brother being the biggest advocate for shoplifting. He had some friends who were avid fishermen. But lures cost money and it's hard to afford them on a teenager's income. These guys worked as caddies at a local golf course and used their money to buy the lures I would steal. I would turn them over to my brother and he would sell them to his friends and then pay me. To this day, I cannot remember what the split was. I guess I was grateful for anything I could get because there was no one else who would buy the stolen goods. It provided me with an income for whatever needs I may have had.

In the 4th or 5th grade I made a few friends. I think they decided to have me for a friend because I was the toughest one in our class. I could beat up anybody in my grade and most of the guys in the next higher grade. My brother was 2 grades ahead of me and I could beat up a lot of those kids as well. It's funny how, even after all these years, I still think in terms of who could beat up who in grade school. One day, my new friends came up to me and asked me to help them because a guy in the next higher grade was picking on them. I rose to the challenge. He was standing by the school building when I went to confront him. He got smart with me and I remember thinking that I could get a two-fer out of him because of where he was standing. I either hit him or pushed him as hard as I could and he flew back into the concrete and brick building and hit his head on the edge of a brick. Blood began to flow and the fight was over. I was proud yet ashamed of what I did. And also a little scared. I expected him to come back after me for revenge. That's what I would have done. But he didn't. Even years later, when I saw him, I was uneasy around him wondering when he was going to make his move on me. It was more of an indication of how my mind worked than a legitimate expectation. I would have held a grudge, nursed it and struck like lightning at the first opportunity - even if it was years later.

I ran into another problem in the 5th grade with a guy a year ahead of me. He took a dislike to me and set out to fight me every chance he got. We were evenly matched although we were opposites in our physical makeups. I was the fat kid with a strong will and a lot of strength. He was lean and muscular like a well-conditioned athlete. He scared me but I fought him again and again. I was relieved when the school year ended and he moved on to junior high school. Our grade school ran from kindergarten to 6th grade, junior high started at 7th and ended at 9th with high school being the last 3 grades – 10th through the 12th.

In the 6th grade I became the intended victim of some of the cool kids in the class. They would gang up on me and beat me up. I couldn't win against six or more of them. They teased me relentlessly and called me names. I suppose some kids would have been intimidated and cowered in fear like a good victim. I got angry and fought back. I laid in wait outside doorways, around corners, anywhere I could get the advantage. My biggest problem was that I was too slow to catch any of them when they were by themselves. If they saw me they could easily outrun me and taunt me all the while. So, I laid in wait and every time I caught one I would beat him up. Sometimes, the other kids would try to rescue my victim - by force or by trying to draw me away. Each time, the poor beaten kid would go tell on me and I'd get yelled at. I tried to tell the teachers I was only defending myself and the other kids started it but they would never believe me. I ceased to care. I learned not to trust any authority figure. They were all against me. I felt alone and isolated most of the time. As I look back on this, it occurs to me that it was my grudge mentality that caused all the problems. Those other kids looked on it all as a lark while I looked on it as a terrible war I must win or die trying.

I made one friend in the 6th grade who was worldly and wise compared to me. He had taken buses downtown and done all sorts of neat things there - shopped at the Moon Fun Shop and went to movies. I learned all about the ins and outs of traveling to downtown Madison on the bus from him. I remember going to see the James Bond movies in theaters with him when they first came out in the 1960s. Somehow, we drifted apart and I never spoke to him after our brief time as best friends.

I was fat until the 6th grade when I decided I would no longer be fat. I was filled with disgust and self-loathing at my gross body. I starved myself. I skipped breakfast and for lunch I would

15

walk about a half mile to a grocery store and buy one candy bar to eat as I walked back to school. Our grade school had a hot lunch program and participation was mandatory. Kids had to either eat the hot lunch or go home for lunch. So I said I was going home for lunch. I lost weight and got taller at the same time. I starved myself so much I probably stunted my growth. I knew nothing about nutrition, and neither did anyone else back in the 1960s. Perhaps I would have done things differently had I known: Exercised, ate protein and got in good physical condition rather than starve myself into skinniness.

Somewhere around this time, my brother and I found a real go-cart for sale. We pooled our money and bought it. We got an engine from a local go-cart track and began hot-rodding around our neighborhood. There really wasn't any place we could legally drive it so we had to play cat and mouse with the local police. It was easier back then than it is now. We also took it up to our old grade school because there was such a large blacktop playground. It had two levels with a paved incline and we could rip and roar all over up there. But it was not really allowed so we eventually got run off. The playground at Crestwood grade school was a kid's paradise. Not only was there a large blacktop area, there was also a wooded area where we could play and a large hillside extending down to a large field. We called the hill the "Battlefield Hill," I suppose because we used to play King of the Hill on it. The field down below was used for soccer - another opportunity to be a bully. I played it like hockey. When I went for the ball, I would charge the kid and try to knock him over to get control of the ball. I was not fast or agile. I used what I had: brute strength.

I also participated in cub scouts over the years. I was often a part of it but not really welcome. I made it into boy scouts and went on a couple of camping trips. The one week-long trip I took was a terrible nightmare for me. I had no friends in the scouts, not even in my own troop. I was still a bed-wetter and peed in my sleeping bag but was too embarrassed to tell anyone so I slept all week in a piss-soaked sleeping bag. No one would stay in a tent with me so I was by myself. My parents came up to see me and I was so ashamed of myself I did not want to spend any time with them. I could not tell them what I was experiencing. There was no communication in our family. No trust. I was alone against the world - a world that caused me nothing but misery and unhappiness. I was incapable of dealing with all the unhappiness in my life and had no one I could go to for help.

TEEN YEARS

By the time I went to the 7th grade the bedwetting stopped on its own. I resolved that things would be different in junior high. There were kids from several grade schools attending Memorial Junior High. The high school and junior high were all one large building with multiple wings and a central area. I started 7th grade the first year the school opened. Had I stayed in school I would have been in the first graduating class that had attended all grades in that school. I found new friends there and a new image. People took me at face value and not as I was in grade school. I was a tough guy and a trouble-maker. I hung out with the misfits from the other grade schools. I found friends who liked me. I was still a bully. I extorted lunch money from other kids and I beat up other kids whenever I thought I had a good reason. I also got a kick out of breaking the school lockers. They had built-in combination locks and if I kicked the handle, it would break the lock. I broke quite a few locks that way. I managed to get passing grades in the 7th and 8th grades but I got worse as time passed. I also started my first entrepreneurial venture.

I was raised a Catholic which included attending catechism every week. I started bringing gum to chew while I was there. Many other kids wanted gum and candy but couldn't get to a store as easily as I could so I started bringing extra gum and candy along and selling it at a profit. I eventually got kicked out of catechism for being such a pain in the ass. The priest acted as if he was imposing a severe penalty on me. I felt like he gave me a gift because my parents wouldn't let me quit but couldn't make me go if the priest kicked me out. Not all priests in the 1960s were perverts. So many people have come forward these days with tales of molestation but I never saw or experienced any of that. The head priest struck me as an old crank with a crazy look in his eye but he never did anything bizarre and wasn't a pedophile as far as I could tell.

My old nemesis from grade school was at the new school to greet me and he wanted to pick up where we left off. He confronted me at school and we met outside after school in a field across the street. There was a big turnout as many other kids came to watch the excitement. I think we fought like this a couple of times. Then he caught up to me away from the school and wanted to fight so we fought again. But every time he went home and told his parents that I kept picking fights with him. I told my side of the story and once his parents found out that he was the person starting the fights they made him leave me alone. Next, another guy a year ahead of me wanted to fight me. I didn't fight him. I don't remember the reason but word got out that I backed down and people said I was scared. Of course, being a tough guy, I couldn't let my reputation be sullied. I challenged him and beat him in a fair fight.

I made friends in junior high. One of them attended a different junior high school. He was a natural promoter and in me he found a fighter to manage. He went around to the tough guys on the west side of Madison - guys in junior high - and set up fights between me and them. We never bet on the fights. It was just a matter of reputation and finding out who was toughest. I won fight after fight. I don't know what is about me that made me win. Maybe it was all the suppressed rage from the years of misery I had as a child. I finally met my match in one guy who fought like a machine. He lifted weights and had a father who trained him. I felt like I was up against a brick wall. The fight occurred at Westgate Shopping Center (since demolished). My manager and I were there while he showed up with a whole slew of supporters who came to watch. I fought hard and long but finally gave up. Later, he told me that he felt the same way about me and was relieved when I quit first. Later, we became good friends and used to fight regularly - real blows but with no malice. One time I moved too slow and his heel caught my chin clicking my jaw shut. It split two teeth which I had to get pulled. For me, it was a badge of honor to lose teeth. It made me feel like I was a battle-hardened fighter.

I ran away from home for the first time when I was 12. I went with Russell and his friend Pete. It was a spontaneous act. We just started walking out of town and hitchhiking. We didn't even look at a map. Pete had a grandma in Wisconsin Dells that he stayed with sometimes so we decided to go there. Each car that picked us up took us a little way. We couldn't go far with them because we were on the wrong road and had to keep changing directions to get where we wanted to go. We finally got there after dark and neither Russell nor Pete had any ideas on where to stay for the night so they decided to call home and get a ride back. I was not brave enough to go sleep in the woods by myself so I went back, too. It irked me to have to call it quits. Maybe it was pride, or a desperate desire for a different life but I didn't want to give up the chance for adventure. However, I had another chance not too much later.

When I was 13 and once again with Pete, we decided to run away again only this time we stole a car. There was a station wagon in a driveway on the way home from school with the keys in it and we took it. Pete drove because I didn't know how. There was an old root cellar where we used to hang out when we skipped school and on the walls Pete wrote some farewells like "Dells Forever" and such. When I didn't show up at home my father went looking for me with Russell as a guide and saw the messages in the root cellar. When we got to the Dells Pete decided we had to check the water in the radiator so we pulled into a gas station and opened the radiator cap and spewed hot antifreeze all over the place. A county deputy pulled in right after that and caught us and took us to the Baraboo detention center located in the courthouse. Our fathers showed up to take us home and I ended up on probation for car theft.

I was pretty determined to run away and made another break when I was 14. Jim and I decided the police were after us for a burglary we did so we took our loot and rode a bus down to Chicago where he sometimes lived. In Cicero, we found a car with keys in it and drove it all the way to Florida. We got caught sleeping in the car on the side of the road and were thrown into Titusville Detention Home. After about 2 weeks there we were extradited back to Wisconsin. They stuck us on a plane and told us not to get off until we were back in Wisconsin. I wanted to get off at a stopover but Jim wouldn't go with me so I stayed on the flight. The first thing my father asked me when he met me at the airport was "what kind of bird doesn't fly?" I said I dunno. He said "A jailbird." I don't know what point he was trying to make but it went over my head.

If I wasn't already on probation, I was when I got back. I spent almost all of my teen years on probation or parole. First, there was county probation, then came State probation. Juveniles were treated very leniently in those days. I had numerous run-ins with the law but the most I ever got until I turned 16 was more probation.

My junior high school years were a steady downward spiral. In the 7th grade I passed all my classes. By 9th grade I flunked every one of them. I constantly confronted my teachers and caused no end of problems for everyone. I had to talk to psychologists, take ink blot tests and school staff were constantly trying to find out what was wrong with me. I couldn't tell them. I lost trust in everyone and everything long before that. There was no way I could or would open up to anyone. The football coach tried to get me on the team but he said I had to cut my hair and I wouldn't do it. I didn't much like gym class anyway so I skipped it most of the time. My real beef was with those embarrassing uniforms we had to wear. I don't think anyone had heard of sweat pants or shorts of the same material. We had to wear tight little shorts made of thin material that barely covered our butts. I put up with it for years in grade school and would no longer do it. The coach finally threatened me once he decided I wasn't going to be on his team. He said that if I messed up any of his athletes he was going to take care of me personally. I forget his exact words but I remember the point he made. It was a non-issue to me. With my new-found fame as a tough guy most everybody wanted to be my friend - including the athletes - so there was no reason to fight with any of them. I was more interested in fighting tougher opponents, guys from other areas I didn't know. I also hated bullies, probably because I had been bullied so much. Every time I would see a bigger guy picking on a littler guy or a girl, I would get enraged and have to stand up for the weaker one. There was an incident back in grade school where my cousin Nancy, who was a few years behind me, was being picked on by some bigger kid. I ran up to him and knocked him down and told him if I ever caught him doing that again I would really beat him up. I suppose that's a bit ironic – being a bully who hated bullies – but nothing I ever did back then made much sense.

I didn't have much luck with girls at my school. The same behaviors that made me popular with the guys turned off the girls. I started going out and meeting girls from other schools to date. I could not see them very often because they lived pretty far away but we would talk on the phone for hours. In the 1960s, most families had one land line and there was no such thing as cell phones or internet phones. I would tie up my parents' phone for hours and when I finally hung up, they would get calls from their friends asking why it took so long to get through. It was a pretty common point of contention between parents and kids back then. My parents didn't seem to mind too much. Maybe they figured that if I was home talking to girls on the phone I was not out getting into trouble. At that age, raging hormones are crying out for release. I wanted to get laid and the girls I was seeing were not ready for that. Oh well, I kept trying.

At age 14 I met Jane and fell head over heels, knee-deep in love. I was smitten. I would have done anything to be able to spend my life with her. For the first time, I had someone who loved me, cared about me. And I got laid! But not really. What we did was make love, not merely have sex. To this day, I still do not know what it was that so completely ensorcelled me. I was awkward and unsure about what to do but figured it out in the end. From my perspective we had a wonderful, torrid love affair. We used to skip school and take turns walking to each other's house. One time she would leave her door unlocked and wait for me in bed naked. I would come over, walk in and join her. The next time she would come to my house.

Alas, I was duped. Jane had previously been seduced by an older guy who had gotten her pregnant and then dumped her. Her mother had to move out of the small town they were living in to get away from the scandal. Jane dumped me. It turned out that she was seeking revenge on all males for what that other guy did to her and I just happened to be the guy who came along. She hurt me to make herself feel better. I was crushed, devastated. I could not stop loving her and following her around like a love sick puppy. I hurt so bad. The only trust I had ever put in somebody had been betrayed.

There was no getting over it. I could do nothing to her and she was through with me. I became bitter, angry and mean. I had to strangle my feelings to stop loving her. I lived only to hurt others and be hurt. The world was there to make others suffer as she had made me suffer. I set out to hurt as many other girls as I could. I would be nice and get them to let their guard down so I could inflict pain - give away some of the pain which filled my heart. I turned as cold and unfeeling as I could. I turned my heart to stone. That was when my death wish first started to show itself. I wanted to live so fast, so hard, so furious that I would end my life in a blazing, glorious death.

Other people do not respond like this to heartbreak, do they? I don't know. As I look back on it over the decades, it seems rather extreme to me now. I could not now imagine ever reacting in such a manner if I were dumped by a woman. I would now forgive her, wish her well and get on with my life.

My life went on but with a different focus. I was 15 in 1969 and illegal drugs were all the rage. Some friends and I decided to try some LSD (lysergic acid diethylamide) to see what it was like. We bought a pill called a blue flat that was supposed to be a 4-way hit - 4 people could get high from it. We split it and took it but nothing happened. The next time we got some orange wedges (I wonder how they came up with these names?) and decided to eat one each. WOW! Let me tell you, that was a trip to another dimension. Acid is not for unstable or insecure people. And of course I was both. I "flipped out," as it was called back then. I had a vision of me being wheeled down an aisle in a hospital on a gurney looking at the lights on the ceiling. I freaked out over that and the fun was over. The rest of the night was a long ordeal of trying to keep my sanity. The other guys kept happily tripping along and I stayed with them but I was in agony. My brain was no longer my own. It was hijacked by the acid. I was sleeping out in the back yard of my friend's house so we could "trip" without our parents realizing what was going on. I went home and got a portable radio, a large one, and carried it with me the rest of the night believing that I was keeping my brain safe inside the radio. We wandered over to a house that was being built behind his house and went inside. There was no light and we had to be very careful not to step into the open hole where the basement steps were to be installed. It was a long night with no relief when the sun rose. The acid just kept on doing its thing. I couldn't tell what was real and what wasn't. I hallucinated for days and kept having flashbacks. My brain was turned to jelly and I felt like an egg beater had been stuck inside my head and scrambled everything up. I felt like the acid had ripped a gaping wound in my forehead and anything could get inside. For years afterward, I had to sleep with a forearm over my forehead to block what felt like an open hole. I was afraid all the time. I lost my nerve. But I was a tough guy so the more scared I got, the harder I had to try to prove I had courage.

Hunter S. Thompson wrote a book in 1967 called "Hell's Angels." I read his glorified version of the Oakland chapter of the Hell's Angels and decided that was what I wanted to be for the rest of my life. I identified with the violence, the wretchedness, the absolute evil which I believed they personified. I set out to be tough enough and evil enough to measure up to them so I could one day become one of them.

Meanwhile, my mother got me a job as a dishwasher when I was 14 at the Memorial Union on the UW Madison campus. She was a food service supervisor in a place called the Rathskeller and used her influence to get me hired. I made $1.45 per hour to start eventually going to $1.65 per hour. This was the heyday of student unrest over the Viet Nam War. There were daily marches by students. The windows in the stores on State Street had been broken out so many times the shop keepers stopped replacing them, preferring to keep the plywood in place for years. I loved to hang out with all the hippies. I worked there for a year and a half and ran away from home twice while I was there. The second time I lost my job.

I used to skip junior high school quite a bit. Sometimes we went to a small wooded area about a half a mile from the school. It was a depression in the earth surrounded by higher ground which could not be seen from the school. There was a fire pit where we built fires and hung out. Other times, we would go to an old abandoned root cellar about a mile from the school. When James Madison Memorial was first built, it was on the edge of Madison, beyond any houses. The closest things to it were a landfill and a nursing home. Everything else was farmland. Now it is surrounded with shopping malls, businesses, apartments and houses.

We also went looking for adventure. One time we found an old Volvo with the keys in it and stole it. We drove it all over the place for a few days. One day while we were out near Mount Horeb, the rear wheels locked up, we skidded and rolled over. My knee went through the windshield. No seat belts, of course. We managed to get a ride to Mount Horeb and began to hitchhike back to Madison. The police found us and wanted to know what we were doing because it was a school day and school was not out yet. We made up some stupid story about why we were there and about how I cut my leg. He took us to Verona to see a doctor and called our parents. We got home all right but after they found the car it was pretty much a foregone conclusion who had stolen it. We got probation for car theft. In gym class one day we were out running to the far corner of the rec field as part of our fitness ordeal and one of my classmates found a driver's license that belonged to an older guy at the school. He offered it to me and I took it as a sign from above that I should start driving a car. So I bought a 1958 chevy for $35. It had no key. Some 1950s cars were made so that you could turn them off and remove the key and keep using the car without the key. The car did have a title, though. I kept it parked across the woods from my parents' house. Every time I wanted to drive it, I would cut through the woods and away I'd go. My parents always thought I was going over to see one of my friends who lived off in that direction. I didn't have much money for gas so we would go out at night and siphon enough gas to get us through the next day. The gas was free and I never had go to a gas station where a cop might notice me. I only had the car a few weeks when I went over to get it one night and it was gone. Somebody had driven it away. I never saw it again. I went out and found a better car. A 1960 chevy for $75. This car came with a key and I put license plates on it. My friends and I drove from the time we got up in the morning until we went to bed at night. Mostly, we cruised around out in the country around Madison. Everything was fine until one night I made the fateful mistake of going to a McDonald's which was the local teen hangout. The police were there, recognized me and asked for my driver's license knowing I was too young to have one. I gave them the other guy's license and while they were checking it out, I ran off and left my car. I figured I was in a lot of trouble for using the other guy's drivers license so I resolved to run away.

This was the first time I left on my own and it was shortly after Jane broke my heart. I pulled my $400 in savings out of the bank and took a bus to Minneapolis. I arrived in the wee hours and the bus depot seemed so uninviting that I decided to just keep on going. I bought a ticket to Seattle, Washington. I rode for days and saw all the sights. I sang songs with some of the other bus riders. There was one old guy who smelled like death and chain smoked. When I got to Seattle, I found the hippie district and hung out there. I really didn't know what to do with myself. I asked around and found someone to sell me some identification - a driver's license - no doubt stolen from its original owner. I met a guy a few years older than me and I tagged around with him for a few days. We hitch hiked out to a big park by Olympia and split up from there. I kept hitching south and ended up in Portland where some middle-aged gay guy picked me up. He grabbed my leg at one point and I was on the verge of stabbing him with my knife when he decided to let me out of the car. Portland was a lonely deserted place on the Sunday when I arrived there. I wrote my parents a letter and made up a story about the gay guy saying he grabbed my leg and I had to stab him to get away. I don't know why I told that lie. Maybe it was to make me seem tougher or more grown up or able to take care of myself.

I kept going south and got picked up by some guys in an old, beat-up car. They were Natives or Mexicans, I'm not sure which. They were good to me. I rode with them to Chico, California and they let me stay with them. But I was restless and wanted to travel. I found a 1956 Mercury and bought it for $75. It had a stick shift, something I never drove before. But I knew how it worked and did okay driving it. I made one mistake with the overdrive. The car had a bad battery and when I left town I forgot to push in the clutch when I stopped and killed the engine. I couldn't get it started again, not even with a push start. I didn't realize the overdrive had to be disengaged to push start the car. I didn't even know what it was for. I just knew it was something you use when driving on the highway. I went back to my car the next day after the engine had cooled off and it started right up. Off I went once again.

I went south until I was tired and stopped in a gas station right off the highway. I went to sleep in the car and got rousted out a few hours later by the police. I knew only one way to deal with police. I started getting loud and threatening. The cop found my knife and a chain belt and arrested me on a weapons charge. I threw my wallet out in a field because I didn't want him to take my money. I went to jail and told a whopper of a lie about who I was. I said I was 19 years old from Cicero, Illinois and had been working on farms and ranches for the last few years and had no identification. I think they knew I was lying but could not find out who I was so they took me to court, gave me 15 days in jail and let me go. I went back and found my wallet; there was still $100 in it. I got my car out of hock and headed south again. This time I had a destination.

I wanted to see my aunt and cousins who lived in Fresno. I had seen them once before when I was 9 years old during a family trip to California. I thought they might let me live with them. I found their house in the wee hours of the morning and pulled up in front and went to sleep in my car. About midmorning I woke up and went and knocked on the door. I sure surprised them. They thought I was a vagrant Mexican. I spent about a month with them. I was happy. They were Jehovah's Witnesses and I went to church with them one time. I even broke one of my own rules and polished my boots before we went. But my father flew out to California and dragged me back to where I didn't want to be. I don't think he could stand the thought that they might turn me into a Jehovah's Witness.

Right before I turned 16, I ran away again only this time I stayed in Madison the whole time. There were so many hippies who ignored the law and would help runaways it was easy to find a place to stay. I would go to grocery stores before they opened and steal the day-old donuts they left outside to exchange for fresh donuts. The bakery truck usually made its rounds before the store opened. I also shoplifted a lot. The parking ramps were a good place to get some quick money. I took a screw driver and popped open the meters and took the change out of them. I never had to go dumpster diving to find something to eat. I would rather steal for my food.

I went out to a small town to live with a guy I met for a couple of weeks just to get out of Madison for a while. When I came back, a friend and I went joy riding in a stolen Camero. We went to his house after the sun rose to sleep and his older sister called the police and had us arrested. They took us to detention. It was the first time I was placed in detention for more than a day or two. I was 16 years old.

The detention facility in Madison had been run by the county sheriff's department. A couple of weeks earlier, it was turned over to another agency which had counsellors instead of jailers. I was angry and determined that I would not stay there. I waited for the right moment and then picked up a table and hit the counselor over the head and took his keys. I locked him in and let myself out. I slipped out a side door and was loose in downtown Madison in my detention uniform. I knew an older woman (19 or 20 years old) who lived nearby and I went to her apartment to hide out. I had a .22 rifle that had the barrel and stock cut down but I had no bullets. I planned on hiding out until I got some bullets and then get a ride out of Madison and live by my wits somewhere else. I waited all day for several people to bring me some bullets. But I guess no one wanted to bring me any because I was so out of control.

After dark, I looked out the window and saw a guy in a suit. I knew he was a cop and knew they were coming after me. It was a second-floor apartment and I went to hide on a porch under a mattress. They crept in and missed me on the first pass. I thought I was home free. But they kept looking and found me under the mattress with an empty gun. This time I was placed in the county jail and at a court proceeding I was adjudged delinquent and placed in the custody of the state until age 21. I was then sent to Ethan Allen School for Boys – a euphemism for juvenile prison.

I hated it. I resented the authority, the rules and having to put up with all the other kids. I knew there was no point in fighting or breaking the rules because I would not get out until I was 21 if I didn't do what they wanted. I went through intake at Ethan Allen School for Boys and then was sent to Kettle Moraine Boys School. Each child is given a potential release date. Mine was set for 5 months after I arrived. It was an eternity. I saw kids who had been in and out 4 or 5 times. They had made a life out of coming to the boys school. They had more friends there than they had in the free world. I did not want to be like that. I had to talk to a psychologist once a week. I didn't realize I was getting therapy. I was just talking to some guy. I had seen so many therapists over the years it did not seem unusual to have someone who wanted to talk to me like that. I took machine shop classes and regular classes. I was pretty sharp in math and helped out as a tutor. We were paid 50 cents per week and could go to canteen once a week to buy penny candy. Lots of kids went and bought their candy and then gambled it all away the first day.

There was a swimming pool and pool tables there. If the guards hadn't been such assholes it could have been a decent place to be. There was an honor cottage where some of the older kids lived. Whenever a kid tried to run away (there were no fences there) the honor guys got to chase him down and subdue him, i.e., beat him up. That didn't happen very often. Most of the time when a guy ran off, he ended up getting sent to the Reformatory in Green Bay (a euphemism for a state prison for younger adults) to be housed with the adults. Someone finally filed a lawsuit over that and they had to return all the juveniles to the boys schools.

My neighbor worked on the trash detail. One day while he was hauling the trash back to the dump he took off. They didn't catch him right away and I never saw him again so I guess he got away for at least a while. My parents came to visit me regularly and I was allowed one friend on my approved visiting list. Debbie is like the sister I never had but she was much more than that. She came to see me and wrote to me which was wonderful.

I got released and got stupid right away. My friends and I got 4 quarts of Ripple wine to celebrate my release and I got drunk and went uptown and tried to get into a bar on State Street near the university campus. The bouncer wouldn't let me in so I pulled a knife on him and then ran off. He called the police who grabbed me on the library mall. I fought and screamed like a maniac while they dragged me away. I went back to the county jail. I woke up the next morning knowing I was going back to the boy's school and I was devastated. I made up a story about going downtown and drinking something from a bottle a hippie had and freaking out from the drugs he had in the wine. Anyway, when they came to get me to take me back to the boys school, I was told that they would give me a reprieve and one more chance.

I met a girl named Jeri who lived on the east-side that I stayed with about a year and a half. She was great! Her mother was an alcoholic who spent most of her time in the bar. When she would come home with her boyfriend, she would often make Jeri sit on his lap. One night I was talking to Jeri on the phone and her mother came home with her boyfriend and made her hang up the phone. I knew what was going on and I got angry. I jumped in my car and raced across town at speeds up to 70 mph (high speeds in town were a regular occurrence for me) weaving in and out of traffic. I got to her house, punched in a door panel, unlocked the door and went in. I commenced to beat the hell out of the boyfriend and when her mother tried to interfere, I pushed her down. I ended up not hurting either of them but the way I exploded into the house and was so angry shook them up. That was the last time her mother ever tried to make Jeri do anything she didn't want to do. I had a terrible temper, no scruples and loved to hurt people. All I needed was a reason. If I didn't have one, I would make up an excuse or pretext to justify what I wanted to do.

I think this was the first time in Jeri's life she ever felt safe. I protected her because in my view I owned her. When she was a couple of years younger she had been gang raped by some guys on the north side of Madison. She was too scared to tell on them but when I found out I went on a rampage. I had a belt made out of a chain and I used it to chain whip other people. I went after these other teenagers with a vengeance.

Another time, Jeri told me some black guys at her high school said they were going to turn her out, i.e., gang-rape her. I was something of a racist back then and I declared war on blacks in Madison. I drove around and every time I saw a black guy I would jump out of my car and threaten him with a pistol telling him to let those guys know I was gunning for them and would shoot them if they didn't leave my woman alone. I was so bold that I even went after one guy on the Capital Square in broad daylight. Now that I look back on it, I wonder if Jeri made it all up just to see me get crazy. My friend Mike, Jeri and I went to

Minneapolis for a couple of weeks in my 1963 Pontiac. I guess we were runaways but we were 16 or so and it was pretty easy to run away at that age. We slept in the car mostly, stayed a while at a group home for runaways but had to leave when we wouldn't let them contact our parents. I worked at a car wash on a day-to-day basis for cash. We lived primarily on bologna sandwiches. One day we were so hungry we called a phone number on a poster which advertised that they would help runaways. We told them we were hungry and they brought us a big bucket of chicken. That was the best tasting chicken I ever ate! Mike and I got our left ears pierced so we would have something to show for our trip. Mike and I had a few unique experiences together when we were teens. We were best friends. He told me about how to tattoo with ink which I didn't believe. I wrapped some thread around the end of a needle and dipped it in some India ink and tried it out. It worked so I put a heart with a jug in it on my arm. I chose the jug because another time Mike told me how to make wine and I used a jug to make the wine in. We got drunk many times on my home-made wine as teenagers.

I started 10th grade but I couldn't stand school. I didn't fit in. My father finally told me I could quit if I got a job so I went to work at Octopus Car Wash. I was there for a year and a half. I spent my money on cars. I had a 1963 Pontiac that I beat to death. Then I got a 1965 Chevy Impala with a 4 speed which I later traded in for the fastest car I ever had. It was a 1966 Ford Fairlane GT with a 390 cubic inch engine and a 4-speed transmission. I drove like a nut. I burned up clutches and wheels constantly. I lost my license numerous times. I went to Florida to stay with my aunt for a month and drove my Ford down there. I drove nonstop from Madison to Miami going around 90 mph most of the way.

The first time I ever smoked pot and got stoned was at the car wash. I never knew what the big deal was about drugs because I had previously tried pot and it had no effect on me. Then when I finally got a buzz, I loved it. I started smoking it regularly. I wonder what it is about marijuana that many people feel no effects the first few times they smoke it? Most of my time was spent working on my car, drinking or getting high and cruising around. One of our favorite pastimes for my buddies and I was to drive around high on pot and laughing at what we saw. I never thought of myself as a worker or a citizen. That was for squares, not for the likes of me. I finally quit my job so I could spend more time partying which meant that I had to get all of my money by stealing. I also thought of myself as a badass. I stole whenever the opportunity presented itself. Then I started making opportunities. I did burglaries and stole cars and motorcycles. Whatever I could do to make some extra money without working. Sunday mornings were house burglary time. We looked for open garage doors with a car gone and we knew the family was at church. We would walk into the garage and bang on the door to the house. If no one answered we would kick in the door and ransack the place. We never got much money or other valuables but I got a kick out of the lawlessness. I became so notorious that the Madison police would watch for my car and when they saw it, they would follow me around. My car was faster than theirs so when I wanted to do something illegal I would ditch them, go do it and show up back in the area I left acting like I'd been there all the time.

My friends and I started a motorcycle club call the Road Knights. When I turned 18, I bought a 1962 panhead for $325 and commenced to be the outlaw biker I always wanted to be. I wore dirty, smelly clothes, never bathed and exulted in how filthy and nasty my "colors" were. Colors were the denim jackets with cut off sleeves that had the club insignia sewn on the back showing who the biker was affiliated with. I was the worst of the lot. The other guys wanted to ride motorcycles, meet up with other clubs and party. I wanted to have wars with other clubs so I could shoot and maim people.

We had a 1950s era panel truck which was our club vehicle that we drove in the winter and used for hauling our bikes when they broke down. One night we had an argument with some guys at a bar and when we left in the van, they followed us. We were cruising down the beltline (Madison's freeway) with these guys behind us. The president of our club was called Mephisto because he had very black hair and very pale skin. He looked like he just crawled out of a coffin. He was in charge and I always obeyed his orders, probably the only person I ever listened to. He didn't want us to fight at the bar so we left. He was driving the van and I told him the guys were following us. I was in the back with a couple of rifles. I pushed open the back doors and was going to shoot up their car but Mephisto told me not to so I had to restrain myself. The guys in the car saw the rifle and decided they didn't want to follow us any more.

Mephisto worked at a bakery and they had flour sacks filled with day-old donuts and other pastries returned from stores. Sometimes we picked him up from work and gave him a ride home. He usually brought a huge sack of the day-old donuts and we would stuff ourselves on the goodies. But we also drove around looking for pedestrians to throw the donuts at. We had great fun hitting people with donuts, not caring what the people thought. One time, Mephisto brought out a cake and we drove around until we found just the right guy to throw it at. He was bending over to light his cigarette and we let him have it. He got so mad and we just laughed. As I look back on it, I wonder how I could have thought something like that was funny. Another time, I was out at a bar with some friends and met a cute woman who was there with her boyfriend. I started flirting with her and her boyfriend got jealous. We got in a little scuffle at bar time and somehow my bottle of wine got broke. I wrote down the license plate number of the car he was riding in. I guess he was the kind of guy who held a grudge, too, because he checked around and found out who I was and learned that I was going to a small motorcycle shop the next day. He found me there and got the jump on me. I was more than a little drunk at the time and he knocked me around to his heart's content. Now it was my turn to go after him. I used the plate number to get the address where I thought he lived and went out there and shot up that house and the neighbors' houses as well. The next day he contacted me and wanted a truce. We met at another bike shop and shook hands. It was all over. Fortunately, nobody got hurt.

I was too extreme even for my biker buddies. We were invited to go on a run with a well-known bike club based in Madison. They were going up to the state park near Black River Falls. I didn't much like them but agreed to go along. I couldn't get my

Harley running in time so I rode up with another guy who was cruising up in his 1957 Ford station wagon. It was a sorta slick looking car. He had the back end jacked up and I assume the engine was beefed up. I loaded up my sleeping bag, tool box and 2 rifles. We generally had a policy of one person staying sober and out of sight of the other club members while holding weapons in case something went down. I was so antisocial and argumentative that I was generally the one to stay out of sight with the weapons. I was also the one most likely to use them and not care about the consequences.

We had a little dog that was our mascot. We had agreed that since he was our club dog anyone who was not a member of our club was not allowed to pet the dog. When we got there one of the other bikers came up and petted the dog. I cussed him out and ran him off. The other guys got mad at me because they were there to make friends with the other bikers, not antagonize them. I said "Fuck that" and in my usual hotheaded manner tore off my backpatch and quit the club. I grabbed my sleeping bag, tool box and 2 rifles and stormed off into the woods to sleep by myself. I was awfully hard headed. I held grudges forever. No forgiving, no forgetting. I watched everyone drive off the next day and then grabbed my stuff and set out for Madison. I decided that I would walk back to Madison if I had to. It was quite a feat because I was more than 100 miles away. I set out walking and hitch hiking. I miraculously got rides all the way back to Madison carrying 2 rifles, a tool box and a sleeping bag. My luck ran out in Madison and I had to walk the last 5 miles or so to get to where I was staying.

Those were crazy times back then. Every day, students were demonstrating against the war in Viet Nam. They would march up State Street breaking out windows and converge on the state capitol. The smell of pepper gas lingered in the downtown area for weeks at a time. It was like a war zone. One day I was sitting on the steps outside the state capitol just hanging out when some people came along and started setting up a microphone near us. Then we saw some guys in suits on the second floor of the capitol setting up a video camera. Pretty soon we could see down State Street where a large crowd was working its way toward the square, battling the police and blocking all the traffic. A large crowd converged around us to hear whoever staged the rally make their speeches. They had their rally and finally dispersed. All the while we were still sitting there. I thought it was so amusing to watch this big demonstration come out of nowhere and go back to nowhere - with nothing to show it ever happened except for us sitting there to witness it.

I broke up with my girlfriend Jeri over something stupid. Somebody told me she was dancing with a black guy at a-bar we were at. I was very racist and used that as a pretext to dump her. I know it shocked and hurt her and it devastated me. I had so much pain in my heart that all I ever wanted to do was hurt others and myself.

Shortly after that, I got caught putting moth balls in the gas tank of a car that belonged to the father of the estranged wife of a friend of mine. I was pretty stupid in some ways. It was easy to send me on a mission. Just tell me any old cockamamie story and I would fall for it. I forget what he told me to get me to do it, but away I went to damage this guy's car who I didn't even know. I got caught in the act and ended up with a year of probation and a $100 fine which I refused to pay. I decided to run off rather than do the probation. I went to Minneapolis to live. I chose that city because I was familiar with it from the trip with Mike and Jeri. I went with a few dollars and not a clue about what I was going to do there or why. I met a couple of guys and they got me a parttime job at a gas station. I then went back to Madison and brought my motorcycle to Minneapolis. It was in pretty bad shape. I was no mechanic and I gloried in driving a junky bike. I was wild and careless and dumped it over on a regular basis. My motto was wire it or weld it. I didn't use bolts. I welded pieces onto my bike or tied them on with wire. By this time I was probably at the worst of my existence. I believed that "might makes right" and whoever is the strongest is the boss. It was all based on physical ability. I loved to drink and smoke pot and then take my cycle out late at night and roar around. I routinely woke up the whole neighborhood and then went out on the freeways. I liked to tease the Greyhound bus drivers I would pull in front of them and flip them the finger or spit on their windshield to get them to chase me. Then I'd try to outrun them. My bike had a top speed of only about 90 mph so I had to do some dodging in traffic to outrun some of those buses. I also liked to take other chances. Whenever I saw a barricade or road construction along the highway, I would see how close I could come to the barricades without hitting anything. I liked to get close enough to let my pant leg brush the barricade. I didn't care whether I hit it or not. I had a death wish and often swore that I would be dead by the time I was 25. I did everything risky I could to make it come true. I guess it was inevitable that I would crash my bike. I was coming off the freeway onto Hennepin Avenue at a high rate of speed. There was a traffic light within a block of the exit and I was going so fast I couldn't slow down when the light turned yellow. A guy coming from the other direction wanted to turn left across my path and when the light turned yellow, he took off. I couldn't stop in time so I tried to beat him through the intersection. He hit my bike by the back wheel and I thought I would be all right but the bike swung around and caught my leg between the car's bumper and the fins of my engine. I flew through the air not knowing that I was hurt, planning to beat up the other driver as soon as I landed. I got the wind knocked out of me as I hit the ground and passed out for a short time. When I woke up, I was face down and my leg felt funny. I looked over my shoulder and thought my boot had come off because the toe of the boot was up by the back of my knee. When I lifted my leg the pain shot through me and I realized that my foot was still in the boot. That was the beginning of years of agony and pain from that injury. At the time I was thinking, "Oh well, I broke my leg. No big deal. People break their legs all the time."

The ambulance came and took me to the hospital. I then saw the exact same lights in the ceiling of the hospital hallway which I had seen during my bad acid trip years earlier. I recognized them and thought to myself so that's what it was trying to tell me. I asked for something for the pain but since I had been drinking that night, they refused to give me anything. They wouldn't operate on me either. I was 18 and in Wisconsin I was an adult but in Minnesota I was still considered a minor. They wanted my parents' consent before operating on me. I wouldn't tell them where I was from so we had a standoff for hours. I don't remember how it was resolved but they finally wheeled me into the operating room and gave me a spinal anesthetic. I went numb from the waist down which was such an unbelievable relief.

The next morning, I woke up in a large charity ward with my leg in traction in a trough. I had so much pain. For a few days I got morphine shots which helped. But then a nurse brought me some codeine pills. I threw them back in her face and told her I used to eat more than that to get high and that it wasn't going to help my pain. From then on, they decided I was a dope fiend and refused to give me any pain medication except aspirin. I ate aspirin until my ears rang but it did no good. The nurse had to check my foot every 15 minutes for a pulse. If the pulse would have stopped, they would have cut off my leg. When they gave me the option of amputation the doctor told me he could remove my leg and have me up and walking on a fake leg in 6 weeks or he could try to save my leg which would take a long time. I told him I didn't care what he did but that if he cut off my leg, I was keeping it. I said I wanted it sealed in a plastic bag filled with formaldehyde so I could hang it in my living room. That way even when I wasn't home, I would still be at home. I thought it was funny but the doctors didn't appreciate my sense of humor, especially since I was serious about keeping my leg.

I spent 3 months in the hospital with my leg in that trough. I had dozens of surgeries. Medical technology in the 1970s was not well advanced. Skin grafts were an experimental procedure. They used the skin from both thighs, my stomach and right hip trying to regrow the missing skin on my lower leg. About 10% of the graft would take. The rest would turn black and fall off. I was a pain in the ass. I bitched, complained, cussed and swore at everybody. I lashed out at anyone and everyone. I alienated every staff member in that hospital. My nickname at the time was "Loser the Boozer" and I hung a sign on my bed with that written on it. I complained so much they finally put my leg in a cast and sent me home in a wheel chair. They inserted pins through the side of my leg and formed the cast over the pins to hold the bones of my leg in place because they still hadn't set the bones. I stayed with a woman I met before my accident. Punky was short and cute and I was attracted to her. She had two small children but I didn't much like kids back then. She had a way of needling me and irritating me so that I'd get angry. I couldn't go anywhere because I was in a wheelchair. Finally, I got on crutches. Then, when I would get mad, I could leave. One day, I got really angry about something or other and decided I wanted to leave her. She got scared and wouldn't let me in the apartment. I wanted to get my bike title before I left. I decided that I would wait in that hallway until hell freezes over if I had to so I could get my title. I slept on the floor in the hallway with my back leaning against her door all night long. The next morning, she finally opened the door to see if I was gone and I pushed my way in hopping on one leg. I grabbed her and slapped her face, back and forth several times. Then I grabbed my title and left. I was shocked at myself. One thing I never did was hit women. It was one of the few rules in my life that was cast in stone.

Everything else I did in my life, no matter how deplorable or depraved, was an acceptable part of who I was as a person. But this wasn't. I wasn't the sort of guy who beat up women. Let me tell you, I am endlessly ashamed of what I did that day. Funny thing, though. Once I slapped her, she became the most loving, obedient, sweetest woman you would ever meet. I couldn't understand that. I hold grudges. I could not forgive her for provoking me until I snapped and hit her. In retrospect, it was my lack of self-control that made me snap, not her actions. She wanted us to stay together and I refused. I left her.

I went back into the hospital for more surgery. They were going to sew my two legs together to try to get new flesh to grow onto my injured leg from my good leg. But when they cut the cast off there was so much staph infection they could not proceed. I ended up back in a cast with nothing done. But when they put the new cast on they changed the angle of my knee. Anyone who has had a joint immobilized for a long time knows that it hurts to stretch it and move it. They set me in a new cast that stretched the tendons and ligaments in a manner that they hadn't been stretched in months and it caused me constant agony. They refused to give me a new cast. I had a knife and tried to cut it off myself. They wanted my knife and I wouldn't surrender it. We finally reached an agreement. I would let them store my knife at the main desk if they would change the cast. I don't know what else they planned for me but I was ready to go. I hardly ever ate the food there. I went in at 150 pounds when I had the accident and was down to about 130 pounds because I wouldn't eat the food. The only time I would eat was when I ordered a pizza and that was seldom since I didn't have much money. One day, I wanted to order a pizza and the nurses wouldn't let me for some reason. I got angry and decided to leave. I bit off the intravenous line running into my arm and got dressed. A nurse tried to stop me from leaving by grabbing one of my crutches. I hopped on one foot and swung the other crutch over my head to keep them away from me. I hobbled down to the main desk and got my knife and left.

It was a cold winter I spent in Minneapolis. All I had for a jacket was a leather biker jacket with no lining. I had to walk everywhere I went. I must have been a pretty pitiful sight because often someone driving by would pull over and ask me if I needed a ride somewhere. I would always take the ride and be grateful for it. But more often than not, I braved the cold and arrived at my destination half frozen. It would take a long time for my cast to warm up after being out in below zero weather with nothing to cover it.

I decided to return to Madison after I escaped from the hospital. I did not want to go there but I really had no other options. It was clear that I would not get my leg fixed in Minneapolis, especially after the way I left the hospital the last time. I needed help. My parents got me in to see a good orthopedic surgeon who put me in the hospital, filled me up with antibiotics and placed my leg in traction. As soon as the infection was under control, he set the bones in my leg and put a cast on it. He ran two rods down the center of the bones to string the pieces of bone together. I was on my way to healing.

There was a particular reason that I didn't want to return to Madison. When I was 17, I had my final confrontation with my brother – or so I thought. When I was in the boys school he had enlisted in the Marines – most likely because he couldn't stand for me to have all the attention because I was away at the boy's school. When I got out, he couldn't stand for me to be at home with our parents. He went AWOL (absent without leave) several times. He was living back at home while he was AWOL and came home drunk every night. He kept wanting me to fight him so he could try out all the new fighting techniques he learned in boot camp. I did not want to but after being away from him for so long I was determined that I would not allow him to dominate me ever again.

One night he lost his house key when he was out drinking and wanted me to let him in so I did. Then he wanted me to give him my key and for me to borrow our mother's key to go get another one made. I said no and he got angry and attacked me. It was about 3 A.M. and we commenced to fighting. Our parents heard the commotion and came running upstairs to break it up. They got between us and I was able to flee. My father hollered to me to call the police which drove Russell into a frenzy. I couldn't find the number and instead grabbed a knife and locked myself into the bathroom. Russell came downstairs and I heard him break the receiver on the phone and pick up the refrigerator and bounce it up and down on the floor. He then threw the kitchen table across the room. He tried to kick in the bathroom door but then must have remembered we had a knife with a broken tip that would work as a key. He got that and opened the door. I felt like I was in one of those scary movies where the monster is coming after you and you are not safe in your hiding place. He tackled me and drove me backward into the bathtub. I stabbed him as I went down. My mother's nose had already been broken by him upstairs and in spite of the injury she followed him into the bathroom to try to pull him off me. My father came in behind her with a one-gallon paint can and slammed it down on his head. My mother tried to block the hit and broke her hand. Russell had previously cut my father's hand with a razor knife when he was upstairs. After I stabbed him, they were finally able to pull him off me and I got up and fled. I saw the phone was broke so I ran to the neighbor's house and called an ambulance to save Russell. I waited outside for help to arrive. The police came and took me to jail while an ambulance arrived to take Russell to the hospital. But he fought them as well and had to be restrained to get him to the hospital. He was one tough son of a gun. After the district attorney got statements from everyone it was determined that I acted in self-defense and I was released. I had only seen him once since the stabbing and was planning on staying away from him from now on. My father had made him go live in Miami with my aunt while I was still living in Madison. But after I moved to Minneapolis, he allowed Russell to come back to Madison. I had resolved after the stabbing that he would never dominate me again. I had no further fear of him. My motorcycle accident changed all that.

Russell had to go back to the Marine Corps and spend time in the brig before he was discharged. Once again, I was vulnerable, unable to defend myself because of my crippled leg. While I was in the Madison hospital he started creeping into my room late at night, stalking me, playing his intimidation game. I learned that while I was in Minneapolis he also went up there to spy on me. I was scared and bought a .32 cal. semiautomatic pistol. I had my leg in traction and kept the gun in the bag which held the traction counterweights.

When I was discharged from the hospital, I was afraid to live at my parents' house with Russell there. I pretty much bummed around staying wherever I could, sleeping here or there. Most of the time it was on the floor of someone's apartment I knew. I was doing this while on crutches with a full-leg cast.

One night I was out at a bar with some friends and ran into Russell. He heard that we were having a party at the place where I was staying and he invited himself to attend. I was afraid to tell him no. He told me to ride with him and I did but I was terrified the whole time. When we got there, he started chugging hard liquor and I felt compelled to join him. We both drank excessively all the time. He got drunk and started randomly beating up on the people there - including me. He would knock me down and stomp on my cast. Other people he would hit or choke as he saw fit. He didn't really stomp anybody into the ground. He was more or less indulging his mean streak. There were a couple of other guys there who could team up and restrain Russell when necessary so he didn't go too far. Nobody liked him being there but they were afraid to ask him to leave. He finally passed out in the living room – or so we thought. Most of the people in the apartment were crowded into one bedroom, afraid to go in the living room. It was a first-floor apartment and the people were climbing out the bedroom window to leave rather than risk going out through the living room. One girl opened the bedroom door to check on Russell to make sure he was still passed out. He sat up when he heard the door. She screamed and slammed the door which made him angry. He jumped up and kicked in the door. I hopped after him trying to calm him down and reason with him.

I still had the .32 cal. pistol but most of the time I didn't carry it loaded. I had an agreement with a guy we used to call Preacher. We were both kind of wild and crazy so we decided that one of us would hold the gun while the other one held the bullets. That way, if the gun was going to be used, both of us had to agree to it. That would prevent me or him from doing anything stupid. That night I had the gun and the bullets because Preacher had to go somewhere. I had the gun in my pocket when I followed Russell into the bedroom. He backhanded me and knocked me onto the bed and went for the girl who was standing by the open window screaming. I pulled out the gun and shot him. He didn't even notice it. I fired at him until he turned and started toward me. When he got close, I hit him with the gun. I thought I had missed him with all the shots and the only reason he fell was because I hit him with the gun. I was scared and sought to leave as soon as possible to get away before he woke up. One of the people who had climbed out of the window ran down the street and found a cop and brought him to the apartment. He arrived just as I was attempting to leave.

I went down to the police station and told the detective everything he wanted to know except where I got the gun. I said a little birdie gave it to me. I didn't know what became of Russell because my mind blocked out part of what happened after I pulled the trigger. I had to take sodium pentothal to regain the memory. I was charged with first degree murder and placed in the county jail. I kept having nightmares. He kept coming after me and I didn't believe that he was dead. I expected him to show up at any minute and get even with me for shooting him. I was an emotional wreck, confused, dazed and in shock. I was crippled from my motorcycle accident and in constant pain, had to face the fact that I killed my own brother and to top it all off was facing a first degree murder charge.

PRISON ONE

I was saved by a young, sharp public defender and my father. Between the two of them they instilled in me a desire to be free and will to live. At first, I didn't care what happened to me. I was finally free of the terror of my life. Nothing else mattered to me. Prison for twenty years? No big deal. Twenty years in prison seemed like a treat compared to a lifetime of fear. I went to trial and the jury convicted me of manslaughter. I had spent several months in the county jail waiting for trial before I decided I wanted to get out on bail. I asked my parents and they found a bondsman who put up $25,000 to get me out for a few months before the trial. When the jury came back with the guilty verdict, the judge sent me home for the night. I returned the next day for sentencing and was given 7 years in prison. The judge stated that I would be eligible for parole in a year and I fully expected to be released after a year.

For the first time in my life, I had a future. I no longer had a death wish. I changed my outlook from intending to die before I was 25 to living to be 100. It was quite a change. Prison was unpleasant. When I first got there, the prison didn't even have hot water in the cells. I got my General Education Diploma (GED) and then went on to get a High School Equivalency Diploma (HSED). I also took a semester of college classes but didn't particularly like it. I took typing classes and became a passable typist. I also took machine shop classes where I made parts for my motorcycle. But the thing that I was most proud of was learning to crochet. The prison had a program which taught prisoners how to crochet. Real men didn't do women's work like knitting and crocheting and I had a perverse desire to learn. I was in prison for killing someone which by my definition made me a tough guy. As a tough guy, you better not say anything about me crocheting or there will be consequences! Well, that's the way I thought back then. Anyway, for my first project, I made a granny square afghan and gave it to my mother. It was the first worthwhile thing I ever did in my life. My mother was shocked and touched. I had never been much of a son in my teen years. I was one problem after another, never did anything good or positive. When I gave her that afghan it made a very great difference in our relationship. I think that was what caused her to forgive me for killing Russell. I also used the proceeds from my knitting and crocheting to order motorcycle parts that I planned to use when I rebuilt my bike after I got out of prison. Many times, it was the thought of getting back on my Harley and riding again that gave me the strength to endure the suffering I went through in there. I contemplated suicide often but never tried to kill myself – mostly because I didn't think it would end my suffering. I believed that even if my body died, I'd live on and still be suffering.

My parents were not talkers. We did not talk about our problems. We never discussed Russell's death. I don't know what they thought because they did not believe in sharing emotions. I learned from them to always keep things to myself.

My leg was still in a cast when I went to prison. I had staph infection and was having trouble getting my leg to heal. I was seeing a doctor in Green Bay who was okay for an orthopedic surgeon but my leg was a special case which was beyond his ability to manage. But he wouldn't admit that so I was stuck getting medical attention from someone who was incapable of giving me the right treatment to heal my leg. I complained and raised a fuss for years but I could not get my treatment transferred to UW Hospital in Madison. My father was a union leader - president of the steelworker's union in Madison. He had a lot of political clout. I told him what prison was like and he in turn went to legislators and others that he knew to force changes in the prison system. One of the things he put in motion was forcing the Division of Corrections to abide by the same administrative rule making procedures that governed other state agencies. Prior to that, the prison system was like a fiefdom unto itself. It operated outside the law and was answerable to nobody. That was changing in the 70s and my father had an impact on how it was changing.

I spent my first year in prison making sure I was good so I could get paroled. When I saw the parole board, they told me I was getting a 12 month defer to be considered again in a year and that I should seek clinical services treatment during that time. I was shocked! I thought what the judge said was what they had to comply with. I wrote to the judge to complain and he wrote me back and told me that if I didn't like the sentence I got, I should have appealed it when I got it and now it was too late. I refused to get any psychological counseling. Not because I didn't think I needed it, but because I didn't trust anyone. I would not reveal the secrets of my soul to just anyone. If I could have found someone I could talk to I still would not have opened up because the psychologists always write down what clients say so others can read it. No matter what, people I did not trust would know my deepest secrets. I would not do that. I resolved then and there that I would have to spend 4 years in prison and resolved to fight the prison system all the way.

I had a desire to go back to the Catholic Church. As a small child, I believed everything I was taught and was a good Catholic. It was only as I grew up that I cast aside all of that as irrelevant. I read the Bible in my cell and was looking for answers. But there was nothing there. My beliefs and feelings did not match what the bible taught. I was empty and dissatisfied. There was no resonance and I felt no connection to the Christian belief system. I felt there must be something wrong with me. How could so many people follow a Christian spiritual path while I was left out in the cold? When I was in the boy's school, I had read some books on occultism and other related subjects. It piqued my interest. I was particularly impressed with Edgar Cayce and the trances where he provided information he could not have obtained by conventional means. However, my interest waned as soon as I got released. Now, I began looking at alternatives to the Christian religion. I read the autobiography of Aleister Crowley and a light bulb went off in my head. Here was what I was looking for. He spoke of a spiritual path based on rational thought and self-direction. He proclaimed we each had a right to determine our own standards of behavior and to live by them. We were not bound by somebody else's belief system. It was up to each of us to discover our own true nature and to live in accordance with that nature. His maxim was "Do what thou wilt shall be the whole of the law." In other words, find your purpose in life and do that to the exclusion of all else. At this time, there was a resurgence of alternate forms of religion -witchcraft, paganism, magick. Many books that had been out of print for decades were being reprinted. I bought all of Crowley's books I could find. I was proficient at knitting and crocheting so I made items and sold them to get money to buy books. I read, studied and meditated. I got in touch with my spiritual nature. I even embarked on an extreme method of mind control (my mind, not someone else's) espoused by Crowley. The teaching was titled "Liber Vel Juorgum" which involved cutting oneself on the arm when a lapse of control over word, action or thought was detected. I was a religious fanatic and set out to convert everyone I met. But as with any fanatic, I was the only one who could see my "vision." What was so clear to me elicited yawns from everyone else. Even though I worked hard to develop my spiritual nature, I did nothing to address my other shortcomings. I had severe emotional problems which I did not address in any way – except maybe to suppress them. It turned out to be a ticking time bomb that eventually went off.

I met numerous dope fiends in prison and they showed me how to do drugs. I was able to self-medicate myself rather than seek out real help. Crowley had also done drugs in his day so I justified it to myself as being part of my spiritual path.

I spent almost 2 ½ years in maximum security. The prison officials tried to send me to medium security and I refused to go. I wanted to go to minimum or stay where I was. They wanted me to transition through medium first. I was learning about prisoner rights and the law. I didn't know much, just enough to bluff. There was a grooming code in prison regarding facial hair and hair length. Five Native Americans were sent to the reformatory for taking over the Gresham Monastery. Their attorney got a federal injunction to stop them from having their hair cut off for religious reasons. When that happened, I drafted a lawsuit alleging a denial of equal protection of the laws and shared it with others. A whole bunch of us filed our lawsuits in the same federal court and the Division of Corrections rescinded their grooming code rather than fight the lawsuits. It was shortly after this that I sent a letter to a prison administrator and told him that I wanted to start a magick study group in the chapel to teach Crowley's system of magick. I stated that if he did not approve it within ten days that I would be filing a lawsuit to force him to do so. Before the ten days were up, I was in minimum security.

While still in the reformatory, I had graduated from a full leg cast to a special brace which could support my weight and hold the bones of my leg in place allowing me to walk. I went from the brace to a cane to walking unaided. I had to have a one-inch lift on my left shoe because my leg ended up shorter as a result of the injuries.

I was sent to McNaughton Correctional Center in Northern Wisconsin. My leg started getting worse again. The staph infection returned. In spite of my objections, I was sent back to Green Bay Reformatory to the same doctor for medical attention. I couldn't get anything done there so I claimed that my leg was all better so I could get sent back to McNaughton.

After I arrived back in McNaughton, I showed my leg to the staff and explained that my leg was not any better but that I could not get any medical attention in Green Bay. They finally decided to send me south to Oregon Farm near Madison so I could go to UW hospital.

By this time, the staph infection was raging out of control in my body. I was suffering recurring bouts of fever and chills as the staph coursed through my bloodstream. I was sick and delirious much of the time. Shortly after I arrived at Oregon Farm, I went to an officer and asked to go to the emergency room. He took my temperature and decided to send me. Once there, I was admitted as a patient and put on a six-week course of intravenous antibiotics to get the infection under control. After spending years in prison, the hospital was wonderful. Because I was rated at minimum security, I was placed in a regular ward with free-world people. A guard would come to the ward to check up on me a few times a day. Other than that, I was on my own. The antibiotic eventually cleared up the infection enough for the hole in my leg to finally close after 4 years. Until then, I was contagious and the doctors put a cast on my leg so I wouldn't infect others with staph. The cast was slightly crooked and placed sidewards pressure on the bones in my leg. I developed a relationship with a nurse's aide while I was there and one day we snuck into the visitor's bathroom to have sex. We did it standing up and I was a bit too energetic and ended up rebreaking my leg. We didn't get caught but when I returned to Oregon Farm I was wearing a cast on my leg. I also applied for assistance from the State Department of Vocational Rehabilitation and after a little bit of fighting with them, they agreed to help me. I became eligible for Social Security Disability at the same time. Between the SSD checks and Voc. Rehab. I was able to afford tuition at a private electronics school that I could attend while still in prison on school release.

I had started leather working as a hobby while at McNaughton. I wasn't very good at it but I liked doing it. At Oakhill, I expanded my operation and began hiring other inmates to make stuff for me while I was attending school. I was stingy and didn't pay them very much but they didn't seem to mind. I was ordering hides ten at a time and had an assembly line operation going on. It brought in a fair amount of money. I continued to fight the administration over whatever issues I could. I was angry over not getting a parole the first time I saw the parole board and all I wanted to do was argue with them when I saw them. At my last scheduled hearing, a few months before my mandatory release date, I refused to see them unless they let me review my social services file beforehand. They said no so I refused to participate in the hearing. In the 1970s, a prisoner's file was considered confidential and the prisoner could not see it. The policy had recently been changed and I was determined that I would see my file. The parole board had denied me release several times already and I was only a few months away from my mandatory release date – the point at which they had to release me because I had served all my time – so it didn't matter whether I received a parole or not. I preferred to spend a couple of extra months in prison to prove a point. I have no idea what point I was making or who I was making it to because the only one I hurt was myself.

I was released after 46 months in prison. It would have been 49 months but I had spent 3 months in the county jail and received credit for that time against my prison sentence based on a new precedent issued by the state appellate court after I was sent to prison. I went to live with my cousin when I was released and I kept on going to school. At first, everything was fine. But I had post-release depression. I thought to myself "I spent all those years in prison looking forward to getting out and now that I'm out, what's the big deal? There is nothing out here for me. Nothing that I want to do or that I care about. I should have killed myself when I first went to prison and avoided all the suffering because there is nothing in the free world to make it worth all that misery."

THE LEFT HAND PATH

I started drinking and smoking pot on a regular basis. The more I got high, the lazier I got. I dropped out of school, started again, dropped again. I was always short of money. I moved to a small apartment on the East Side of Madison. I decided that I would rather risk going back to prison than be broke all the time so I started selling drugs. I ate acid (LSD) again; tried cocaine, opium and pharmaceutical drugs. I rebuilt my motorcycle using the parts I had made while in prison and rode that all over the place. I still had a cast on my leg. I kept rebreaking my leg because I would not slow down long enough for it to heal. Eventually, it healed but it took a long time. I met a woman named Linda to whom I was attracted. She was a dietetic technician at UW Hospital and had a nice car. She liked to party as much as I did. I think I fell in love. Something about her touched my heart.

We started living together and took a 2-week vacation in her Z-28 Camaro. We went east to Pennsylvania and then south down to Florida and over to New Orleans. It was a fun trip. She got pregnant and we decided to get married. When I got my Wisconsin driver's license suspended for driving like an idiot we moved to Colorado after the wedding where I could get a Colorado license. I also quit selling drugs but I realized I could not make a living with only half an electronics degree. After about 6 months, when my Wisconsin driving suspension was over, we returned to Madison. My father got me a job working 2nd shift as a grinder at the foundry where he worked and I went back to school full time to get my associate's degree in electronics. I studied and when I wasn't working or in school, I sold drugs. I did it for a year and graduated. I would have been better off working more hours and not doing or selling drugs but I could not cope with reality without getting high. It really messed up my judgment and priorities. But at the time I was clueless.

My daughter was born shortly after we returned from Colorado. It was the most spectacular moment of my life. I was right there in the delivery room and when the nurse put her in my arms, I felt such love for this little person who was looking around with such wide eyes. This was the one person I truly loved and cared about. I would do anything for her.

My belief was that I could live my life as I saw fit and that since I was doing my Will, I would get whatever I wanted. But I was deluded in my perceptions. I was following the Left Hand Path. That's a term occultists use when referring to a person who is not seeking spiritual attainment but rather selfish ego-centered power. When I first discovered my spiritual nature in the Reformatory and began my spiritual path, I swore a solemn oath that I would spend my life dedicated to the Knowledge and Conversation of my Holy Guardian Angel. I followed it for a while but I heard the siren call of earthly pleasure which lured me from my path. I gave lip service to my commitment but no dedication. Among those who follow a spiritual path which involves Ceremonial Magick there is really no such thing as Black Magick or White Magick. Many of the procedures are the same. All that distinguishes them is the intent of the magician. Acting with pure intent according to the dictates of your Holy Guardian Angel is White Magick. Placing the desires of your ego above all else and seeking gain through ritual is Black Magick. Needless to say, White Magick never involves destruction nor harming anyone or anything nor seeking to control others against their will. White Magick involves the use of ritual and ceremony solely to achieve spiritual enlightenment. I thought I was doing the right thing when in fact I was following the Left Hand Path. I spiraled down into evil as a way of life. I had a mean streak which I indulged frequently. I could not see my situation clearly because I was too busy sating my sensual urges and desires. I did whatever I wanted whenever I wanted. I had no regard for others and no empathy. I was different from who I was before Russell's death. Then, I was bent on hurting and being hurt for its own sake. Violence was paramount in my life. Afterward, the rage and drive to hurt was gone. I no longer sought out excuses for violence for its own sake. I looked on it as a sometimes-necessary solution to situations. It was an improvement but I had a long way to go and didn't know it. I also stopped being a racist while in prison. I came to realize that skin color was irrelevant. It is what is in a person's heart which determines what kind of person he or she is.

One guy owed me some money for some drugs he got from me on credit and I put some pressure on him to pay me. He got scared and his solution was to set me up with an undercover agent to get me busted. I made one sale but got suspicious and wouldn't sell to him anymore. Besides, he wanted cocaine and I dealt with very little of that. Cocaine was overpriced and didn't have much of an effect. When I told the agent that I quit selling drugs and was moving out of state as soon as I graduated to start a new life, he hatched a plan to bust me. Rather than let me go scot-free to start a new crime-free life, he wanted to make sure he got credit for his undercover work by arresting me. They came up with a devious plan to arrest me. They knew that a six-month-old warrant for a single sale of LSD would not put me away for a long time which is what they wanted. They also did not have enough evidence to get a search warrant. So they had someone call my house and warn me that the police were on their way over to my house with a search warrant in order to trick me into leaving my house with all my drugs. It worked! I fell for it. I went for the Hokey-doke. The police were waiting for me outside of my house and planned to stop me before I got out of the driveway. I went out my back door and jumped into my truck and turned around in the parking lot behind my house so I was driving forward toward the street. The police did not realize that I would be coming out facing forward and expected to cut me off as I slowly backed out of the driveway. I was out and gone before they could pull in front of the driveway to block me. I turned the first corner and sped past an unmarked squad car parked in the middle of the road. The cop driving the car jumped out and tried to stop me by holding up his hand. By this time, I knew I was set up but it was too late to do anything about it. I planned on driving just far enough ahead of them to dump my drugs out the window and then pull over. But I took a corner too fast and the drugs spilled out onto the floor of my pickup where I couldn't reach them from the driver's seat. I was racing along Northport Drive with the police in hot pursuit trying to figure out what to do. I approached a stoplight where another squad car had stopped all the traffic and blocked the road with innocent bystanders. There was barely enough room between a telephone pole and a junk car being towed by a wrecker for me to squeeze past the roadblock. I got by but my rear tire caught on the junk car and blew out. I spun into an open field, unable to go any further. The officer behind the road block then came bouncing out in the field where I was stopped and rammed the right side of his squad into the front of my truck. He then pulled away and circled completely around and rammed the left side of his squad into the front end of my truck. He then pulled his gun out and pointed it at me. I smiled at him and raised my hands. My pursuers finally caught up and swarmed the vehicle playing their tough-guy game. They yanked me out of the vehicle and threw me down and ground the side of my face into the pavement. To be honest, I didn't take it very seriously.

I appeared the next morning in court and the judge set a $2,500 bail on the drug charge with a signature bond and a $200 cash bail for the traffic violations. The detectives were livid. They wanted me put away without bail. I hired the same attorney I had for the murder trial in 1973. He had gone into private practice and specialized in drug cases. I told him the story about how they tricked me out of the house and caused the high-speed chase. He called the prosecutor's office and told them what the police did. It changed everything. They had to tread carefully to keep their own complicity in creating an unnecessary high-speed chase out of the public eye.

While I was out on bail, I got a job in Freeport, Illinois working for MicroSwitch as an electronics evaluation technician. I hated the job but took it because it was close enough to Madison that I could return for court dates. I found a 5-bedroom house out in the country near Davis, Illinois for $175 per month. It was a great place to live except for a pig farm across the street. A couple of days a year when the wind was blowing the wrong way we would be polluted with the stench of pig shit. Otherwise, it was no problem. The landlord was a decent guy. He offered to sell the house and lot to me for $20,000 and I turned him down. I didn't mind renting a house across from a pig farm but I didn't want to own one there. I told him I'd buy it if the buildings across the road were included but he couldn't do that because his other tenant was raising pigs there. This should have been a wonderful time in my life. In some ways, it was. I loved my daughter. The farmhouse was large and pleasant, especially in the summer. I had a wife who loved me and a good job as an electronics technician.

Yet nothing pleased me. Nothing was good enough for me. I took off on my motorcycle every chance I got. I drank alcohol every day and smoked pot on a regular basis. I also ate psychedelic mushrooms, snorted cocaine, and dropped acid. I was always seeking more money, more thrills, and more excitement in my life. I hated my job, I hated being married. I felt like I was trapped in my marriage and I wanted out.

I made numerous trips back to Madison for court dates on the drug charges. I dragged the proceedings out for as long as I could. Finally, my attorney got me a plea bargain for 4 years probation, 30 days in the county jail and 360 hours of community service. It was a very good deal and very hard to get. The probation officer who wrote the presentence investigation report (PSI) included numerous unfounded allegations and activities. All of it was hearsay. My attorney objected and the judge ordered a new PSI to be written. I then hired my own social worker for $500 to write a presentence report to refute the lies told by the probation officer. I raised the money to pay for the social worker by selling a photo ID machine I had planned on using to create fake Colorado driver's licenses. I bought it at an auction and the only reason I didn't follow through in my plan was that I forgot where I put my old Colorado driver's license which left me unable to get forms printed up to use with the machine. The assistant prosecutor in charge of the case was angry that I got off so easily. Then I was given the opportunity to do the county jail time at a later date to be determined by the prosecutor. I stalled as long as I could and finally spent 30 days in the Stephenson County Jail in Illinois. I had daily Huber privileges and free time on the weekends with my wife and child. By that time, I had alienated my wife so much that she didn't even want to come to pick me up on the weekends. But I insisted so she did.

After I finished the jail time, I declared that my reputation was ruined in Freeport (where I worked) and promptly quit my job because of it. I left my wife and child and moved back to Madison. I helped Linda move to Belvidere where her job was and gave her all the household furnishings. Leaving her devastated me but I couldn't help myself. I held a grudge against her for something trivial which occurred right after we were married and I couldn't let it go. She told me she had an inheritance coming when she turned 21. We were living in Colorado when she turned 21 and I kept pestering her to get the money so we could get a fresh start there. She called home and after talking to her mother, told me the will had been changed and she wasn't getting anything. I suspected she knew it all along and had just been stringing me along. I decided she lied to me just to get me to marry her and I resented her for it. I held a grudge about it. I had been a successful drug dealer in Madison but had quit selling drugs and moved to Colorado to start fresh leading a law-abiding life. I had counted on using her inheritance to get us started on a new life. I did not have a degree and couldn't find a job which paid me enough for us to live on and Linda was pregnant and couldn't work. We finally sold off a bunch of our stuff and moved back to Madison to stay with my parents. I destroyed our marriage. I blamed it on my wife but it was my fault. I was not happy and all I cared about was what I wanted. I cheated on her numerous times, did whatever I liked and in general was an ass. Lots of drugs and alcohol made it seem all right. As with so many things in my life, looking back on it now, I don't know why I thought it was the right thing to do. I hurt so badly leaving her. I was feeling so lost and lonely without her. But I steeled myself, suppressed my feelings and left. I didn't want to leave my daughter with her. I wanted to keep Santina. But I knew with my terrible record and unstable lifestyle I could never get custody from a court. I wanted Linda to agree to let her come to live with me. Maybe if she would have, I would have gotten a job and a place to live and been more responsible. I like to think so but probably not.

Instead, I helped Linda move to an apartment near her job and went back to Madison - the last place I needed to be. I quit my good job at MicroSwitch and got a job at a small electronics firm in Madison where I had previously worked when I was attending electronics school. That lasted only a few weeks. My boss fired me because I only showed up when I felt like it. Who can blame him? He wanted a technician on the premises to fix the equipment that customers brought in. I wanted to come and go as I pleased.

I had developed a side business while I was in Illinois which I continued after my return to Madison. My mother liked to go to flea markets to set up a stand and sell the glassware that she picked up at garage sales. She would often buy an item for 50 cents or a dollar and get $20-30 for it. She knew what was and wasn't valuable in glassware. I went with her a few times and brought along leather goods which I had made. I sold a bit here and there. While still living in Illinois, I saw an ad for cheap jewelry from a place in Chicago and decided to drive down there to check it out. I spent about $100 on earrings and took them along at the next flea market. People came to admire the leather goods but bought the earrings. I sold out almost all that I had bought. A light bulb went off in my head. I saw a chance to make some money. I started hunting up wholesalers of jewelry and other items and buying in bulk and then selling it at a hefty markup. Flea markets were not very good compared to other opportunities. I learned how to register for county fairs and festivals and any other place where people come to have a good time. For an average of $100 per fair I could get 15 feet of frontage space to set up my stand for 5 days. I sold my goods until the crowds went home and then slept in my van. I had a fawn-colored Doberman that someone had given me as a pup. He had been lost out in the country with a cast on his leg. Nobody knew to whom he previously belonged. I took him in and we became virtually inseparable. I trained him very well so he would heel, come, stay, etc. He guarded my van for me at the fairs and when I shut down for the night, I would take him out to romp in the fields with me before we went to sleep in the van.

After I was fired in Madison, I started drawing unemployment based on my MicroSwitch job. I decided I wasn't going to pay rent and spent an entire winter living in my van. It was fun. I had to sell my dog because it was too cold for him in my van. I had a cot and a kerosene heater. I did just fine. I used to joke that I would never have to worry about getting picked up for drunk driving because I had my bed with me wherever I went. If I was too drunk, I just went in the back and fell asleep until I was sober. After the coldest months passed, I bought my dog back. The guy only wanted him to breed with his dog and since he got that done during the winter he was glad to sell him back.

I was aimless in the spring of 1984. I was doing nothing worthwhile. I was mostly drinking, smoking pot, and taking other drugs. There were so many things I could have been doing. Yet I chose to squander my life in a haze of drugs and alcohol. I had lived with my cousin, Lyle, when I first got out of prison. He was a very likeable guy. He was involved in all kinds of shady deals and always managed to avoid getting into major trouble. I admired much about him, especially his talent for talking people out of their money on one pretext or another. We rarely planned our meetings. We just sort of ran into each other randomly and went out and had wild times. At this time, Lyle had a girlfriend who owned a house up in the Wisconsin Dells area. I had gone up there a time or two to help him remodel her house. But their relationship soured and she kicked him out or he left - or something. And Lyle had another woman, Shirley, who was an old business associate - she worked for him when he ran an escort service in Madison years earlier. Shirley lived in Sun Prairie and Lyle began staying there, sleeping on her couch. Shirley loved cocaine. She struck me as someone who would go with whoever had cocaine but maybe I misjudged her. Shirley had 3 kids (2 of them living with her), not much money and no job. Lyle had lent her a car to use while he was living there. After a few weeks things became strained between them. I don't know the details. Perhaps I should have taken more interest in what went on between them because their relationship changed my life forever.

PHOTOS

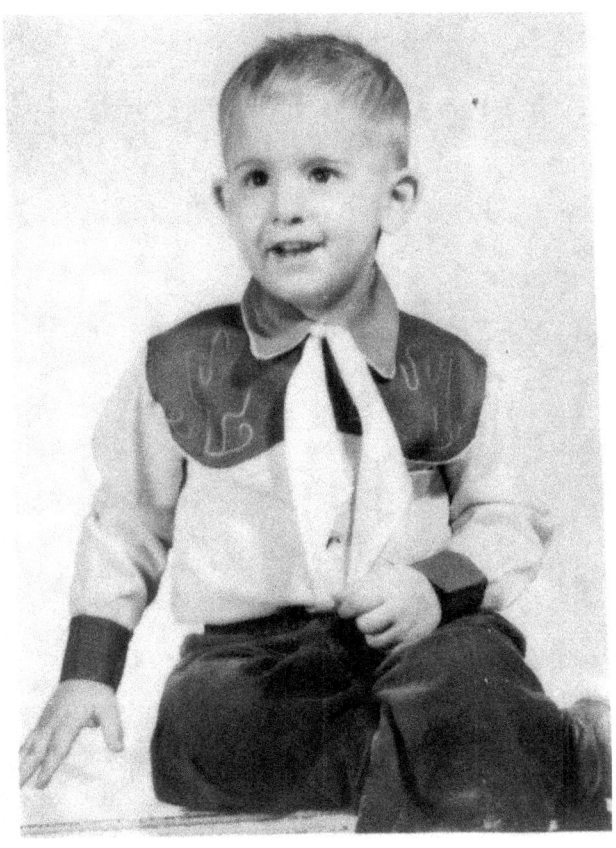

Photo of me, late 1950s, probably 2 or 3 years old.

Here I am, pudgy and smiling, circa 1963 (9 years old).

MAR 1968

Shooting pool in my parent's basement. You can see that by the time I turned 14, I was evolving into a tough guy/delinquent.

I'm posing on Russell's Triumph motorcycle in 1968. He let me sit on it, but would never let me ride it.

APR • 70 •

Typical photo of Russell taken in 1970, which would have made him almost 18.

Courtroom break during my 1973 murder
trial with my parents.

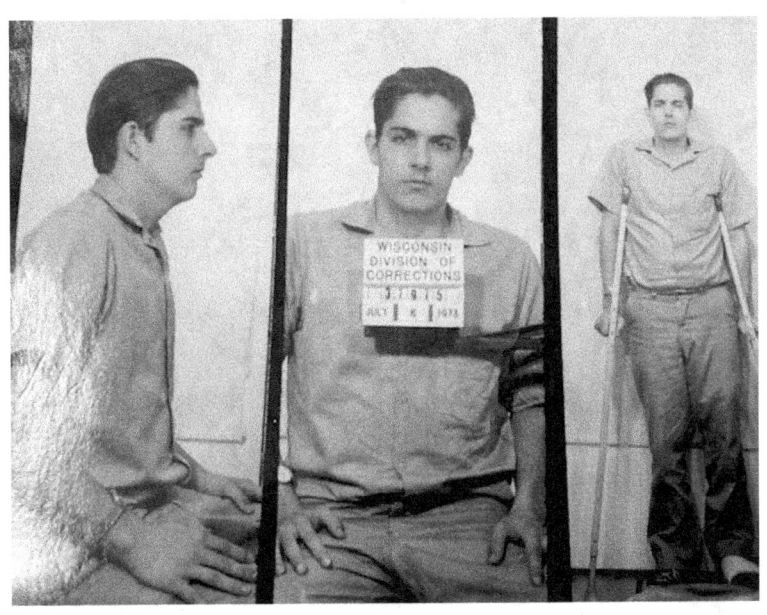

July 1973 intake photos at Green Bay Reformatory – since renamed Green Bay Correctional Institution.

Posing with my dog – Geburah – early 1980s.

Living in Davis, IL early 1980s, while working at Microswitch.
I sat my daughter on my motorcycle for a photo op.

Earley 1980s. Counting money at my jewelry stand with
friends hanging out in the background.

Early 1980s, sitting in front of my van at a county fair –
I don't remember which one.

Early 1980s. I'm wearing the leather hat I made for myself
while sitting at one of the fairs where I set up to sell jewelry.

NAME	RICHARDS, Harlan C.			NO. 37975-A	D.O.B. 01-17-54	INST. DCI	SECURITY Max	DATE 12-15-87
HEALTH Left Leg Amp.			OCCUPATION Electronics		RECOM'ZD WCI		RECALL. 6	
Tech Disable 1st ≈ 200								
CRIME								

First Degree Murder with use of a Dangerous Weapon (Repeater)

TERM Life (Less 1 Week CJT)				COUNTY Dane
DATE RECEIVED 11-09-84 DCI		PAROLE ELIG. 01-25-96	M.R. DATE N/A	DISCHARGE N/A
WARRANT ☐ YES		DATE	REASON OK Security by law	

* DCF ASSIGNMENTS AND VISITS

DATE	DEPT.	RM.	DATE	DEPT.	RM.	DATE	DEPT.	RM.	DATE OF VISIT	HRS.	USED	LEFT	DATE OF VISIT	HRS.	USED	LEFT
11/9/84	New	R-17	1-14-86	School	P-36	8-24-87	IN	F-1								
10/9/84	I.S. Ctr	L-8	3-05-86	I.M.U	P-36	9-02-87	PSW	N-8								
11/1/84	Recep	U-17	3-31-86	School	P-36	10-24-87	PSW	I-27								
		R-29	3-07-86	School		10-29-87	SCHOOL	P-4								
12-4-84	Rec'd	R919	3-31-86	School	P-36	12-27-86	7LU	P-4								
		U1	5-31-86	School	A-316	3-6-88	SCHOOL	P-4								
1/2/85	WCI		4-04-86	School	C-31											
1-02-85	IN	G-6	1-07-87	School	P-18											
1-12-85	IN	F-15	3-16-87	IN	P-18											
2-13-85	EMC	F-15	3-20-87	School	P-18											
7-24-86	School	N-50	3-24-87	7LU	HC-35											
9-18-87	School	P-36	4-10-87	7LU	HC-27											
12-12-88	OCI	DAW-C2	4-13-87	PRC	P-7											
12-06-88	School	P-36	4-29-87	UNAS	P-7											
12-18-88	OCO	Dane	5-27-87	UNAS	D-45											
			6-13-87	UNAS	F-1											

☐ SECURITY OFFICE ☐ SOC. SERVICE SOC. WORKER *RICHARDS, Harlan* C-150

Prison record detailing the first few years of my imprisonment.

Feb 1988

1988. Family photo of my parents, daughter and me at a prison banquet after being sent to prison.

Fox Lake Correctional Institution mid-1990s, posing in my cell with a leather binder that I had made.

Late 1990s, after my father had passed away. My mother, her
cousin Jack and me on a visit at Fox Lake.

"Billy," one of the dogs I helped train in 2008 while I was at
Sangar Powers Correctional Center.

Gordon Correctional Center in 2010, where I worked as a state
van driver and was allowed to wear my own personal clothes.

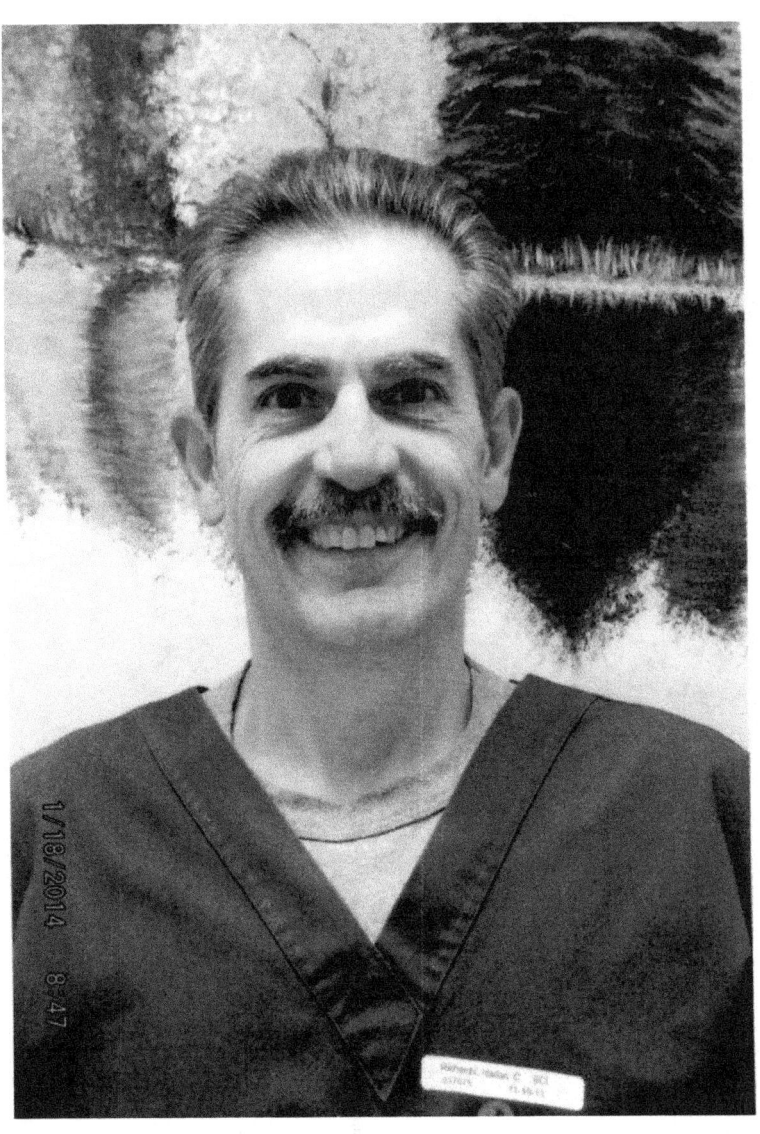

Stanley Correctional Institution in 2014 at age 60.

One of my final prison photos taken in 2020 when I received
a certificate from Chippewa Valley Technical College for
completing a Microsoft Office course.

THE HOLY SPIRIT DIRECTS
MY STEPS

One fine April evening in 1984 I was cruising in my van on the east side of Madison and saw Lyle just as he saw me. We pulled over, talked for a while and decided to go out partying. I parked my van with my dog in it and we took off in Lyle's vehicle. At the time he had a small pick-up truck that was overdue on its payments. He was driving it until the repo man found it and repossessed it. I have no idea whose name the truck was in.

We hit a few bars, raised a little hell and ended up at the union hall - a place I had the keys to because my father was the president of the union and I used to go there to help him out occasionally. There was a private bar in the basement with tap beer so we sat around drinking a couple of beers. Lyle called Shirley and then wanted to go out there. I didn't feel like it but the night was still young and we had nothing else to do so off we went to Shirley's apartment. We got there a little after 1 A.M. We brought a pitcher of beer with us and commenced to enjoy ourselves and play loud music. Shirley seemed ill at ease but I paid it no mind because Lyle was so off-the-wall most of the time that I never knew what was going on between him and others. It was none of my business so I didn't care. Shirley got a phone call and went off by herself to talk. After a while we started bugging her to get off the phone and talk to us. Lyle told her he was going to pour a pitcher of beer over her head if she didn't get off the phone. The person on the other end hung up and Shirley stated that Ron said he was coming over. Lyle got upset about it and I said to relax: If they're friends of Shirley's, they're friends of ours.

But Lyle had some information he didn't bother to share with me. For one thing, the reason Shirley was acting so strange around Lyle was that he had hit her a week or two earlier and she was afraid of him. He also failed to mention that he had met Ron a few days earlier at Shirley's apartment and that Ron had kicked Lyle out of Shirley's apartment telling him not to come back. Lyle had even been telling Shirley and God knows who else that I was his enforcer and that I had been to prison for killing someone. Shirley may have feared Lyle but she probably feared me more because I was a killer who she thought was at Lyle's beck and call. Shirley, of course, had told Ron all about Lyle, what Lyle had done to her and what Lyle had said about me.

There I was, the only one not knowing what was going on. I thought we were having a good time waiting for one of Shirley's friends to show up and party with us. Shirley thought she was in danger from Lyle, and Ron thought he had to rescue Shirley from Lyle and me. I have no idea what Lyle thought. We sat around and kept on listening to music. We ate some ribs, drank some beer. About 3 A.M. I finally said, "Let's go Lyle, nobody is coming." Just then there was a knock on the door and 2 large angry, mean-looking men entered. It was Ron and his big brother Dick, there to rescue Shirley.

Lyle was in the kitchen eating ribs, Shirley was standing in the dining room and I was standing in the hallway at the entry to the kitchen. Ron came in first heading straight for Lyle. As he passed, I said "Hi, my name is Harlan, I'd like to shake your hand." He ignored me and went to confront Lyle. Dick walked past me and I repeated my introduction and made the same offer to him. He slapped my hand out of his way and walked past me. Ron asked Lyle what he was doing there when Shirley had asked him to leave. We both said nobody asked us to leave and Shirley also piped up that she had not asked us to leave. Meanwhile, Dick was pacing the living room floor working himself into a rage. He was mumbling to himself, getting angrier and angrier as he walked. Shirley then suggested that we all go into the living room and sit down.

Ron kept Lyle cornered in the kitchen and kept talking to him. Dick, still pacing, urged Ron to hurry up. Finally, I heard him state "I came here to kick some ass and I'm going to do it." I thought he was referring to Lyle and I was wondering how to defuse him without getting involved in a fight. As Dick walked past me, I repeated my gesture and offered again to shake hands with him. I had no idea that I was the "ass" he was going to kick. Having grown up with a volatile, violent older brother I knew that often times you can distract someone bent on violence if you can get them talking. Once they are talking, if you don't provoke them further, they will not explode into violence. But, because I did not know that Lyle told Shirley I was his enforcer,

I was unaware that Ron had brought Dick out for the express purpose of dealing with me. Ron had recently served time for attempted murder. He was on parole and had just narrowly escaped being revoked for choking a woman he was dating. The only reason he was able to stay free was that the hearing examiner concluded his victim was too unstable to testify against him. In the attempted murder charge, Ron had used a shotgun to try to kill a rival for his ex-girlfriend. She had dumped him and started dating someone else. He could not stand losing her and invaded her home intending to kill the other man. The guy jumped out a second story window to save his life. Ron remained, sexually assaulted the woman and held her hostage for hours.

The entire family was steeped in violence. Dick had a 20-year history of unprovoked attacks on people he didn't know. I did not recognize him at the time but after I heard his name I knew him by reputation. He was the enforcer for the Endres family, arguably the most violent and dangerous man on the West Side of Madison. He led a reign of terror wherever he went. Those who knew him were careful never to cross him. Those who didn't know him soon learned to fear him. Dick was about 5' 10" and weighed about 235 pounds. He had some fat on him but a lot of muscle.

Dick sucker punched me when I offered to shake hands with him. I didn't expect it at all. I was knocked back by the force of the blow. It dazed me and I was confused. Dick came after me as I staggered backward trying to stay on my feet. He was swinging lefts and rights at me. I back-peddled into a darkened hallway that led to the bedrooms and the bathroom. It had a dogleg shape and I bumped up against the wall. It was what held me up as I sidestepped along the wall trying to get away from Dick. He grabbed me by the lapels of my shirt and coat to keep me from going any further and began to hit me. I started hollering to "Get this animal off me." I have no idea whom I was calling to. Maybe I expected Lyle to get away from Ron and come to my rescue. I blocked Dick's blows as best as I could and tried to think of what to do. I was scared, dazed and confused. I couldn't break his grip on my lapels. I knew it was only a matter of time before Dick hurt me badly. He was much larger than me. I weighed only 150 pounds and had a crippled leg as well. I felt like a rag doll in his hands. I always carried a knife. I used to sell knives at my stand and carried one so I could use it as a sales pitch in regarding the quality of the blade. I would tell how I could cut ropes and boxes, strip wires and whittle without ever dulling the blade. The knife was small, only having a 3" blade. Not much of a knife. I never dreamed it was possible to cause a man's death with such a short knife. But I guess I never gave it much thought. I figured it was a short knife and I couldn't get in too much trouble with it because I couldn't do very much damage with it. I pulled my knife and stabbed Dick in the arm that he was holding me with. I was reluctant to stab him deeply for fear of hurting him too badly. It was dark in the hallway and he did not see the knife. Neither did he feel it. I stabbed him several times there with no result. I went lower and stabbed him shallowly in the side. I didn't want to hurt him, just get away from him. After a couple of wounds, he realized I had a knife and hollered: "Ronnie, come help me, the fucker's got a knife." Then he started fighting harder and trying to disarm me. I expected him to back off and try to get away from me when he realized that I had a knife. And I was willing to let him get as far away as he wanted because that's all I wanted. But he had different plans.

I panicked. Oh my God! I couldn't even handle this one guy and there is another one coming to help him who was just as large and just as angry. I began slashing frantically at Dick - his head, his arms, his face - wherever I could reach him. He was unfazed. He kept on fighting, grabbing for the knife. I knew I had only seconds before the other guy was going to show up to help him and I had to get loose from Dick. He gripped my wrist with the hand holding the knife and began to force my arm to the ground and me along with it. When my hand was only inches from the floor and I was on the verge of being thrown to the ground, I made one last desperate jerk of my arm and broke his grip. Fear lent me strength and speed. Dick's hand was bloody from a hand wound which made his grip less firm and that was all that allowed me to break free. As I pulled my wrist loose from his grip, and before Dick could react, I swung my arm up over my head and came down on his shoulder striking behind his collarbone and down into his chest. It caused him to hesitate for a fraction of a second and I followed in quick succession with several more blows to his chest. The blows finally took a toll on him. He stopped attacking me and then started to fall backward. But his left hand still held on to my lapels with an iron grip as he tried to drag me to the ground with him. I put both hands on his wrist and pulled and pulled. He would not let go. Finally, I gave a desperate wrench on his wrist and broke his grip. I looked up and saw Shirley in the hallway and Lyle standing behind her.

I called to Lyle, "Get me out of here." He said, "Follow me," and turned and walked out of the hallway. I stepped over Dick and staggered past Shirley careening off the wall. As I looked out into the living room there was Ron blocking the way with a knife in his hand. Just when I thought it was over I had to take on another attacker! I knew there was only one way out of that hallway. I had to go through Ron to get away from Dick. I advanced on Ron with the bloody knife held in my hand in front of me and told him to "Back off!" He backed off as I advanced and we circled each other in the living room. All I wanted to do was get out of there and I was angling toward the door. Lyle had already left. As we circled, Dick came staggering out of the hallway hollering that he had been stabbed. He went from a violent, brutal enforcer to a crying, beaten man in a matter of minutes. Ron looked over toward Dick and when he turned his head, I fled out the door. I was so weak from the shock and the already-existing weakness of my bad leg that I collapsed on the lawn outside the apartment. My legs simply gave out. Lyle was ahead of me telling me to hurry up and I was struggling to get up and run. I followed him the best I could. We drove off.

We went back to where my van was parked and changed vehicles. My Doberman was in the van and I couldn't leave him unattended for too long. I cleaned up the blood and changed my clothes. We took off heading south. I was scared and didn't know what to do. I had no intention of going to the police. In my life, the police were always the bad guys. They couldn't be trusted. We drove down to Illinois. I don't remember how far we went. After a while I calmed down. I had a chance to think things through. I had done nothing wrong. I was the victim. I was attacked by a raging maniac and defended myself. I hoped the guy was not too badly hurt. I didn't think he could have died from the wounds. He was up and walking and hollering when I last saw him.

We turned back toward Madison and I stopped to call the only attorney I knew – the same one from 1973 and 1979. I trusted him completely. He had defended me when I shot my brother and again when I was facing drug charges. When I had no hope and didn't care what happened to me after my brother's death, he helped me to fight the charges and avoid a long prison term. Trusting him was my undoing but I had no way of knowing it at the time. I met with my attorney while Lyle met with his attorney, Dan Linehan. We told them exactly what happened. At least I told my attorney what happened. I assume Lyle did the same with his attorney. My attorney said that as far as he was concerned it was a who-dun-it until the police came up with evidence of me stabbing Dick. I turned myself in to the Dane County Sheriff's Office with my attorney at my side. I had feared they would shoot me on sight if I came in alone without any witnesses. My attorney told me not to answer any questions so I refused to talk to them. They placed me in isolation for not answering the booking questions. I expected to see my attorney right after I was booked. After several hours I finally agreed to answer the booking questions so I could see my attorney.

Dick bled to death from the stab wounds to his chest and I was charged with first-degree murder. I couldn't believe this was happening to me. It was my worst nightmare. After 5 days, I was released on $35,000 property bond put up by my parents. It is amazing how many sleazy, lying scumbags there are in a county jail. After only 5 days, where I said nothing to anyone about what happened, two jailhouse snitches came forward with fabricated stories about statements I allegedly made to them about the stabbing.

My attorney hired a retired police detective who had originally investigated the 1973 shooting of my brother when he was a Madison detective. Now he was on my side. Or so I thought. My attorney asked me if I objected to him. I had nothing against him. Little did I realize how he felt. He was still smarting about me avoiding a murder conviction in 1973 and set out to make up for it in 1984. It was another fateful error on my part. The now-private investigator was the one who first proposed the contrived defense to my attorney.

He went out to the apartment to look around and noticed a pool of blood outside on the sidewalk. He wanted to know what it was from. I had no idea. It wasn't there when I left. My attorney was still intent on the "who dun it" theory of defense. Under discovery, we eventually got all the statements made to the police. Lyle and I had both refused to talk to the police based on the advice of our attorneys. Shirley told exactly what happened and Ron made up a story about me shoving Dick to start the fight. Ron then went on to claim that he ran down the hallway when Dick hollered for help, saw me straddling Dick when Dick was down on the ground and kicked me to dislodge me from Dick. Ron went on to claim that he then got a knife from the kitchen and ordered me out of the apartment.

The police were rightly confused. Had Lyle and I gave them statements about what happened, rather than take the advice of our attorneys, I probably never would have been charged with murder. Instead, the police staged a "reenactment" with Ron and Shirley which ultimately led Shirley to change her testimony just enough to support Ron's lies. Shirley was emphatic in her police statements: Ron never went down the hallway past her. At the trial, Shirley testified that as she turned her head, she felt this whooshing and that it must have been when Ron went past her. It was just enough corroboration for Ron's lies to be believed by the jury. Instead of Ron being exposed for the coward he really was he came out looking like a hero. Ron had to lie; he was on parole after serving time for attempted murder. Had he told the truth his parole would have been revoked and he would have been sent back to prison.

Meanwhile, the detective and my attorney were busy cooking up a defense based on the "who dun it" theory. They decided to use the pool of blood outside of the apartment to argue that someone stabbed Dick outside of the apartment other than me. Namely, Lyle. They wanted me to testify that I ran outside with Dick chasing me where Lyle attacked him and inflicted the fatal wounds. There was a missing kitchen knife and the pool of blood to support their theory of defense. The private detective was the one who thought up the story and conveyed it to my attorney. My attorney trusted his judgment and wanted to present it as a defense. I objected. I did nothing wrong and wanted my day in court to vindicate myself.

My attorney gave me several good reasons for going along with the story. Most important was that he said my prior manslaughter conviction would be brought in to the trial if I relied on self-defense. If that happened, I could expect the jury to convict me regardless of the evidence because I was a two-time killer. They also told me about a trial where my attorney had recently gotten his client an acquittal based on a similar deception. The defendant had testified that he had thrown his knife into a lagoon. After the pathologist testified about the nature of the stab wounds, the detective came in at the last minute with a knife he claimed to have pulled out of the lagoon where the defendant threw it. The wounds, as described by the pathologist, could not have been caused by the knife the detective had recovered. Instant acquittal. Implicit in this description was the fact that the detective waited until after the pathologist described the wounds so he could come forward with a knife that did not match the wounds in order to secure the acquittal for their client. My parents had paid my attorney $20,000 to defend me. It was their entire life savings. My attorney told me it was the only defense he would present for me and that if I didn't go along with it, I could go to another attorney and he would keep the retainer. I felt I had no choice.

He was the only thing standing between me and my worst nightmare. I wouldn't dream of going to trial with anyone else. My attorney had an almost mythic quality about him in my eyes. I believed I would get justice and be vindicated with my attorney at my side. I didn't really care what method he used. If he wanted to mislead the jury as a means to get me the acquittal I deserved, then I would help him all I could.

First, my attorney wanted me to get Lyle out of town for the trial. Lyle had not cooperated with my attorney during his preparation for the trial. It was inexplicable. Lyle should have been eager to help me. But he didn't trust my attorney so he wouldn't give my attorney any of the information that he needed regarding the background of Shirley. My attorney wanted Lyle to disappear, so that's what I had him do. Next, my attorney hired a blood expert to testify that the pool of blood could only have been caused by someone standing there and bleeding outside of the apartment. Finally, he wanted me to recruit a credible witness to testify that Lyle and I met with that person after the stabbing and that Lyle admitted stabbing Dick outside of the apartment. That way, it didn't matter what lies Ron told because our story would be so different from his that the jury would have a reasonable doubt. I would be acquitted; for the wrong reasons, but acquitted none the less. If they tried to convict Lyle of murder, all the evidence they would have is my claim that he did it while their witnesses were saying that I was the killer. Another acquittal based on reasonable doubt.

The stabbing happened in April and the trial was scheduled for the end of October. I did what my attorney asked - found a witness and made sure Lyle would not appear at the trial. It was a tense six months.

The Endres family came from the West Side of Madison, not far from where I grew up. Even though I did not recognize them the night of the stabbing, when I heard their names afterward, I knew who they were based on their reputations. They were renowned for their violence and dangerousness. There were very few people who grew up on the West Side of Madison who did not know and fear the Endres family. Dick was the worst of the lot. He was the one that the others went to when they needed help. That night in April was no different. Except for the outcome.

Ron wanted to get back at me but was afraid to come after me himself. He lived 3 blocks from my parent's house where I was staying while I was out on bond. He sought other ways to get at me. He had heard that I was dating a woman who worked at a bar called Off the Wagon located in Monona. He set out to get me through her. He didn't know who it was, only that it was a dark-haired woman who worked there. Meanwhile, my girlfriend quit bartending there and another dark-haired woman was hired. Ron had a friend, a fellow Viet Nam vet named Steve Garrard who was a sexual predator. He had served prison time for rape in the past. Back then, there was no sexual predator law and nothing to keep him in prison after he had served his time. He was living in Ron's basement. Ron took him to Off the Wagon and struck up a conversation with the bartender. He persuaded her to accompany Steve and him to a party after the bar closed. However, Ron stopped at an apartment, claiming that he had to pick something up. But he came back to the car and told them he was staying and to go ahead to the party without him. In reality, there was no party. Steve took the woman to Ron's house and persuaded her to stop in for a moment before they went to the nonexistent party. Once he had her there, he brutally raped and tortured her for hours. She broke free at one point and ran for help. But he caught her and dragged her back inside. She finally convinced him that she would go to the Veteran's Hospital with him to get him help. His time in Viet Nam had twisted him up inside and made him the predator that he was.

As soon as she was free of him, she called the police. The police caught both men in Ron's car when Steve went to pick up Ron and drive him home. At first, Ron was implicated but when it became known by the investigating officers that Ron was the star witness in my murder trial, everything was hushed up. Ron's house, Ron's car, Ron getting the two of them together was all kept quiet and Ron's involvement was kept out of the investigation results. Within a couple of days after this, the prosecutor filed a motion for a speedy trial. She had to get the trial over before Ron did something else. I received word through a mutual friend that Ron was responsible and that he thought it was my girlfriend. A poor innocent woman was brutalized in an attempt to sate Ron's thirst for vengeance. What would I have done if he had gotten my girlfriend? I don't know.

There were other incidents during that summer where different members of the Endres family tried to get at me or get my bond revoked. None of it was successful. I was self-employed as a vendor at county fairs and other special shows. I spent most of my time traveling from fairgrounds to fairgrounds selling my goods and making the most of my freedom. I was in denial. I didn't want to face the trial or the chance that I might go to prison for life. I wanted it to all go away. It didn't matter what I wanted. The trial arrived.

We chose the jury and the prosecutor put on her witnesses. Ron lied as expected, Shirley changed her story to match Ron's story as expected. Shirley's two children, too young to really know what they were saying, came up with some outlandish stories of their own. In their statements to the police, they saw nothing.

After the reenactment they both had a lot to say on the matter. My attorney did very little cross-examining of the witnesses. He didn't bother to impeach them to the extent that he could have. He exposed the reenactment and Shirley's change of testimony but left Ron's past and his motive to lie unrevealed to the jury. My attorney kept telling me it didn't matter. It all depended on the pool of blood outside of the apartment. As long as the prosecutor did not bring in testimony in her case in chief about the origin of the pool of blood, the contrived story would work. Any testimony on rebuttal would look like a fabrication by the State.

Well, sure enough, the last witness to testify was a paramedic who explained that the pool of blood was caused when Dick was shifted from one stretcher to another and the excess blood was dumped off the original stretcher. There went my attorney's fabricated story. Now what?

We met that evening in my attorney's office to discuss the next step. My attorney asked me what I wanted to do. I told him that I wanted to do what I always wanted to do: tell the truth and rely on self-defense. He asked where Lyle was and I told him I didn't know. I followed his order and had Lyle disappear for the trial. I wanted him to ask for a continuance or a mistrial so we could get Lyle to the trial. My attorney refused to do so saying he would have to tell the judge what he had planned and he was not going to do that.

As I look back on it now, I believe that the private detective was the one who tipped off the prosecutor on the last day of the trial about the pool of blood. He guided my attorney into setting up the contrived story and then destroyed the only piece of evidence supporting the story when it was too late to develop a legitimate defense. I think my attorney acted in good faith at all times. But I have no proof, only suspicions and circumstantial evidence.

Well, the rest of the trial was a travesty. I got up and told the truth which made very little difference to anyone. With Lyle gone, I had no credibility. All the prosecutor had to do was ask the jury if I was telling the truth, why wasn't Lyle there to testify. She didn't stop at that, though. She engaged in every bit of shady conduct she could possibly get past the judge. Even with all that, it still would not have been enough to persuade a jury beyond a reasonable doubt had not the judge jumped on the bandwagon. He crafted the jury instructions to ensure a conviction based on the evidence. The first thing he did was create an instruction which incorporated the shove alleged by Ron as a fact: "If you find that the defendant provoked a fight by engaging in unlawful conduct in shoving Mr. Endres, he is not privileged to resort to the use of force intended or likely to cause death or great bodily harm to Mr. Endres unless he reasonably believes he has exhausted every other reasonable means to escape from or otherwise avoid death or great bodily harm at the hands of Mr. Endres." It made the shove an undisputed fact and left it to the jury to decide if it was unlawful conduct which took away my right of self-defense. Next, he told the jury they must stop deliberations once they found guilt on first- or second-degree murder. Under the law, if they found facts to justify a murder conviction, then they were required to determine if there were mitigating factors which would require a lesser conviction for manslaughter. The jury was so confused over the instruction they asked that the testimony about how the fight started be read back to them. In the end, though, they found me guilty of first-degree murder.

The judge immediately sentenced me to life in prison. I was angry. I got hokey-doked. I blamed everybody but myself. As I look back on it all, I can now see I put myself in prison. Every time I had a choice to make, I made the wrong one. Every time there was a crossroad which led either to prison or an acquittal, I chose the path to prison. My flawed judgment was equally devastating to my numerous appeals.

At my first meeting with my attorney after my conviction he was sympathetic to my plight. He offered to do my appeal for free. I told him I wanted him to give back $5,000 to my parents and I would get someone else for my appeal. If he didn't, I would reveal what he planned to the court. He refused and I exposed him.

I met a guy in jail who knew a lot about the law. Teddy Lee Heffner had his own law books and shared them with me. I told him all about my attorney and what my attorney had did to me. I used his law books to draft my own post-conviction motion and filed it in court. The public defender refused to appoint counsel to represent me unless I withdrew my pro se motion. I had no choice. Even though I read enough in the law books to see I got shafted by my attorney I was not able to represent myself in post-conviction proceedings. The PD's office had to find private counsel to represent me because one of the jailhouse snitches/liars was currently being represented by a public defender and it would have been a conflict of interest to represent me as well. It turned out that neither snitch/liar was willing to come forward to testify at my trial without being able to do so anonymously but their statements had allowed the prosecutor to cross-examine me during the trial about the lies they told. Then, to make things worse, Teddy Lee Heffner contacted my trial attorney and claimed that he helped me make up the story about why Lyle was absent from the trial. He said that he would testify to that if my trial attorney agreed to represent him in his pending criminal cases. The attorney refused but wrote memos to himself about it and submitted them to the court to discredit my claim. It worked!

I went to Dodge Correctional Institution for about 3 months. It is the intake facility for people who get sent to prison. Prisoners are evaluated and analyzed to determine which prison they should be sent to. In my case, being 30 years old with a life sentence it was a foregone conclusion – Waupun Correctional Institution (WCI). There were only 2 maximum security facilities besides in addition to the reception facility at Dodge: Green Bay Correctional Institution (formerly the Reformatory) for young men and Waupun for everyone else.

I never believed for a minute that I would serve very much time on the life sentence. I was clearly not guilty of murder and just as clearly, I did not get a fair trial. I expected to be back out in a year or so and planned accordingly. Then the delays started. First, it was getting an attorney, then it was waiting for transcripts, after that it was scheduling conflicts for my hearings. All the while, I was in the law library reading case law. I bought my own set of statute books and read them cover to cover. I sent my appellate attorneys letter after letter. I got my own copy of the transcripts to study. I did everything I could to aid in my appeal. I was so naive. I thought that the judge would hear the evidence and base his ruling on the facts presented. I did not think of judges as human beings - people with biases and beliefs that influenced their decisions. Many people knew what my attorney did to my defense. My father, Lyle, Lyle's attorney, my coached witness, and I all testified to what my attorney did. None of us had a chance to prepare, rehearse or compare our stories. It was essentially five different sources all saying the same thing. The judge had the choice of accepting the truth and destroying a prominent attorney's career or leaving a two-time killer in prison for a life sentence he most likely deserved. Which would you do if you were the judge and had worked with the attorney for years?

I was disappointed with the judge in denying my motion for a new trial. Surely the appellate court judges would see through the cover-up by the trial court and grant me relief. I just knew that there was no way a Wisconsin Appellate Court would leave an innocent man in prison because of what his attorney did to him. Wrong again. My post-conviction attorneys were competent, able lawyers. They did everything minimally required to represent me. I finally realized during the appeal that that is what they were there for: to give me legally competent representation while ensuring that my murder conviction stayed intact and my attorney's reputation stayed unsullied. All this time I had been studying the law. I worked in the prison law library and had begun filing lawsuits against the prison administration on various issues. I was learning but I was far short of being capable of representing myself.

There was one issue regarding the jury instructions I wanted my attorneys to raise relating to the offense of manslaughter. The judge misstated the instructions which prevented the jury from considering whether I should have been found guilty of manslaughter instead of murder. My attorneys wouldn't raise it and I was not capable of doing it on my own. But I decided that I would rather have my fate in my own hands than that of attorneys I thought were selling me out. I fired them and went pro se. Another one of my bold moves which ensured that I would serve life in prison. I was naive enough to believe that the appellate court would reverse the murder conviction of a pro se defendant if he deserved a new trial. I believed that the courts existed to see that justice was done. Not in Wisconsin. Maybe I would have had a chance in California where people like O.J. Simpson can buy their acquittal. In Wisconsin, the criminal court system exists solely to enforce the power of the State. It does a very good job of it. To reverse the conviction of a pro se killer would undermine the very thing the court system exists to protect - its own power. Judges are merely attorneys with black robes. They could not, would not, accept a pro se, self-taught prisoner's legal arguments and rule in his favor against a licensed attorney. I lost my appeal.

I then went to the State Supreme Court on a petition for review. At that time there were 4 conservative judges and 3 so-called liberal judges. The liberals were called that because they believed in protecting the rights of the citizens. The conservatives had kept a lock on the court for years. No criminal defendant had a chance in that court. If one was lucky enough to win in the appellate court, the Supreme Court would grant review in order to reverse that decision. Ex-governor Tommy Thompson was a master at maintaining control of the State Supreme Court. Every time a conservative was going to step down from the court, he retired early enough so that Thompson could appoint another conservative knowing that the incumbent running for the supreme court was a sure bet for re-election. It worked well for him for years. I lost every step of my direct appeal. I could have filed a petition for a writ of habeas corpus in the federal court right then but each defendant only gets one chance in federal court. I wanted to make sure I had everything in front of that court when the time came. I had been in prison 3 1/2 years and realized it was going to take me a lot longer to get justice than I had first figured. I settled in to win a long, drawn-out war.

I knew that Dick Endres had a reputation as a violent, dangerous person. I had heard vague references to things he did but did not have any of the facts. At the trial, the prosecutor misrepresented him to the jury as a family man of good standing in the community. My attorney knew the truth. The judge and prosecutor knew the truth. Everyone knew the truth - except me and the jury.

I set out to get whatever evidence I could on Dick's past. I sent a request to the Crime Information Bureau for information and they sent me his rap sheet - page after page of arrests and police contacts. Most of the records were from the Madison Police Department so I sent them an open records request for all arrest reports concerning Dick. At first, they didn't answer me but I persisted. I threatened legal action if they did not respond. They finally sent me a letter telling me I would have to pay them $100 in advance for them to begin to process the request because there were so many reports on him. I thought they were bluffing just to get me to abandon my request figuring that I would not send them $100. I sent the money and a few weeks later I got a stack of police reports along with a letter telling me to send them another $100 if I wanted them to send more documents. So I did. I ended up with a stack of reports about a foot tall concerning Dick's police contacts. He had a 20-year history of unprovoked attacks on people he didn't know. The exact same thing he did to me!

I also made an open records request to the State Historical Society to see if his old prison records were available. They were but I was told I had to prove he was dead before I could get access to his file. I thought it was kind of ironic that I was serving a life sentence for his death yet had to prove he was dead to get access to the documents. I got them and they showed more of his volcanic nature and destructive acting out as a way of life.

I was pretty sure that the prosecutor had all the information about Dick so I made an open records request to the Dane County District Attorney to gain access to the closed prosecutorial file in the murder case. They ignored my request so I filed a writ of mandamus in the circuit court. The court ordered him to turn over the documents and he refused. The judge ordered that a fine of $100 per day be assessed against him until he surrendered the documents. He appealed and the appellate court stayed the imposition of the fine until the appeal was completed. It took the court of appeals a year but they agreed with me and once again ordered the documents to be turned over to me. The State Attorney General filed a petition for review to the state supreme court, which was granted.

The case went before the State Supreme Court. It was all briefed and awaiting a decision. At the November election that year a Democrat, Jim Doyle, was elected as the Attorney General. As soon as he took office, he petitioned the supreme court to dismiss the petition and leave the appellate court decision intact as the controlling standard on access to closed prosecutorial files. The Supreme Court refused to dismiss the case and a few weeks later issued a decision reversing the appellate court and overturning 20 years of prior case law to deny me access to the documents I needed to show that I did not get a fair trial.

The conservatives ruled against me and the liberals filed a dissenting opinion. It was a bad precedent and set back the cause of open access to government records a long way.

I had all the documents I could obtain under the open records law so I began to prepare my post-conviction motion. At the time, there was case law which allowed a defendant to seek a new trial at any time based on constitutional error. It had been the settled law of Wisconsin for decades. I relied on this to present my issues regarding Dick's past and the jury instruction error. The trial court sat on my motion until the Wisconsin Supreme

Court issued yet another draconian decision. State v Escalona-Naranjo created a procedural block to stop any defendant from filing a claim if the claim was known at the time of the direct appeal and not raised in the appeal. My motion was denied on those grounds. For the second time, 20 years of prior precedent was thrown out causing me to lose my chance for a new trial. I appealed the decision trying to argue that the procedural bar should not apply retroactively. I also filed a habeas corpus petition in the court of appeals arguing ineffective assistance of counsel because my attorneys refused to raise the jury instruction issue while representing me. My habeas petition was denied almost immediately. Later, when my appeal was denied as well, the court did agree that I was denied a fair trial by the use of the faulty jury instruction but that I had procedurally defaulted on the issue and could not get relief. The court then went on to say that if I wanted to challenge the conduct of my appellate attorneys I should have filed a petition for a writ of habeas corpus with the appellate court to reinstate my direct appeal!

There are no motions for reconsideration allowed in the appellate court so I filed my petition for review with the State Supreme Court. Part of my argument was based on the hypocrisy of the appellate court in denying my habeas petition and then telling me I should have filed a habeas petition if I had wanted to raise the issue. A few days after my petition was filed, the appellate court issued an amended decision deleting the language regarding the filing of a writ of habeas corpus. This change allowed the Supreme Court to deny my petition - if not with a clear conscience at least with a clear record.

I was finally ready for my federal habeas corpus. But during the years it took me to get through the state courts a second time the federal Congress passed the Anti-Terrorism and Death Penalty Act which rewrote the standards for federal habeas corpus actions. There was a new deferential standard of review which prevented the federal court from granting me any relief. There was a virtually identical jury instruction issue out of Illinois which had been addressed by the Seventh Circuit Court of Appeals and which allowed numerous Illinois prisoners to get new trials. The federal court refused to apply it to me. In order for a state prisoner to prevail on federal habeas corpus he or she had to cite a U.S. Supreme Court decision on the issue. Since my jury instruction issue had only been decided by the Seventh Circuit Court of Appeals, I was denied relief. I lost on all levels. There were many published federal court decisions which should have entitled me to relief but the new standard barred their consideration. More than a dozen years after I was wrongly convicted of murdering Dick Endres my conviction became final. I had to accept that I would be serving a life sentence and would only be released if I earned a parole.

Had I known in 1984 that I would end up serving a life sentence, I probably would have taken my own life and avoided all the pain and misery I've endured over the years. Nothing is worth this much suffering. But by the time I had to face this reality I had already spent too many years in prison. To end my life at this point would have made all the previous years of suffering meaningless. The biggest heartbreak of coming to prison was leaving my 5 year-old daughter behind.

I knew she felt betrayed, hurt, and abandoned. Even now as I write this, it brings tears to my eyes. How she must have suffered over the years. All the promises I made that I was coming home soon. I was so sure I would be vindicated. To this day, she refuses to have anything to do with me or even speak to me.

Filing my appeal was not the only thing I did while in prison. I became a renowned jailhouse lawyer. I spent years in my cell writing, typing and filing legal actions against the Department of Corrections (DOC). I would sometimes type for 12 hours straight. It was my major activity for most of the time I was in maximum security. I won some cases, lost many others and developed a reputation.

I also became a political activist. There were inmate groups in the prison and I joined the European Culture Group (ECG) and Lifers Group. Soon, I was chairman of the ECG. I ran that group for two years and then became president of the Lifers Group. We made contacts with community activists and coordinated our activities. Many times, we worked together to derail regressive litigation or seek publicity for wrongful actions of the DOC. When a lifer died without any family after 47 years in prison, we took up a collection and bought him a headstone and issued a press release. We were intent on not being shut away in prison and forgotten.

I became a fitness fanatic as well, lifting weights, running, and playing handball. My crippled leg finally began to heal properly and get strong. I was still disabled but I overcame many of my mobility limitations. I also quit smoking. In the late 1980s college courses were introduced into the prison. I earned a 2-year Associate of Arts and Science degree.

I spent 8 ½ years in maximum security. Over the years, I had tried many times to get transferred to medium security. I won numerous court actions but they were all pyrrhic victories - victories which, even if you win them, are meaningless. All the courts had the power to do was reverse the decision and remand it back to the Program Review Committee (PRC). Each time I won a new hearing the committee members would get angry and deny me again. I finally gave up hope of ever getting transferred. I was despondent, at a loss and didn't know what to do. In 1993, I met my social worker for the pre-PRC interview and she told me to stop arguing with the PRC members. She said to just keep my mouth shut and let them make their decision. Since there wasn't anything I could do to persuade them to approve me it didn't matter to me whether I said anything or not. So I finally went to a PRC hearing and kept my mouth shut. The PRC could not reach a unanimous decision and they referred me to the second step process. I didn't bother to get my hopes up. I knew I had antagonized all the DOC officials in Madison so badly that none of them would approve me on a split decision. The months rolled by. I had forgotten that a decision was still pending. It didn't matter because I wasn't going any place anyway. About 3 months after my hearing, I got my written PRC decision. I was in shock. I was approved for transfer to Fox Lake, a medium security facility. They cited my excellent conduct record as the basis for the transfer. I immediately wrote to my social worker to ask her where I was on the transfer list. She told me I was number one. Four days after receiving my PRC decision, I was in Fox Lake.

I RECOVER MY SPIRITUAL PATH

I was in a daze. After all those years living in a 10 x 5 foot cage and rarely ever leaving it, I was at the most wide-open medium facility in the state. Another guy and I had arrived together. He had been there before and knew the ropes. The guard told him to show me where Unit 3 was as he was assigned there as well. We checked in with the officer who issued us keys to our rooms and told us what wings we were in. I asked the officer what I was supposed to do now. He said he didn't care as long as I got out of his office.

What a difference from Waupun! In Waupun, every guard watched every inmate. We did not come out of our cells unless we were authorized to be at a particular place at a particular time. We had to be under escort while moving in a group or carry written authorization (called a "pass") to go anywhere. At Fox Lake, we pretty much had the run of the whole place. It was like an all-male college campus. There were more guys than jobs so unless I actively searched for a job it would take several months before my name came up on the seniority list and I would be assigned to a job. I decided to take advantage of the opportunity and kept my mouth shut. I was allowed to keep all my leather hobby materials in my room and I could sell finished leather items to other prisoners. I love working with leather and I spent many hours making belts, purses, wallets and multitudes of other items. I became quite good. I developed an eye for color and learned to airbrush dyes on leather.

Recreation was open from 8 a.m. until 8 p.m. except for meal times and counts. There was a huge recreation field and an unpaved jogging track. I lifted weights and played hour upon hour of handball. It was so quiet and relaxing to be able to go out by myself on the huge rec field or to walk the track all alone. It gave me many opportunities to think.

I finally got drafted to work in the prison kitchen. The kitchen job was not that bad. All I did was show up at meals and stand in the serving line dishing out food. As soon as I started working, I signed up for the "safety course", a 6-week program which was a prerequisite to working at Badger State Industries (BSI). There was a wooden furniture factory which paid more than regular prison wages - up to $1.00 per hour. I had no intention of ever working there but I took the safety course just in case it would come in handy later. And it got me out of the kitchen. I decided to continue my education and get my bachelor's degree while at Fox Lake. I intended to use Pell grants and grants from the Wisconsin Higher Educational Aids Board to pay for it. I managed to complete my first 18 credit contract with grants at Fox Lake. I was assigned as a school student and studied in my room. The only time that I had to go to the onsite school building was to take the exams. But there was a public outcry over prisoners getting grants to go to school so the U.S. Congress took Pell grants away from prisoners. I lost my funding and the university would not allow me to continue until I paid my tuition in advance. Desperate times call for desperate measures.

I had been making a lot of money from selling leather to other inmates but at around the same time the DOC banned inmate-to-inmate sales of hobby items. They claimed that hobby sales were being used to mask drug sales. It wasn't true but DOC administrators will not listen to others once they make up their minds about something. With that source of income gone, BSI was my only option. I got hired at BSI as a stock room clerk making $1.00 per hour. I borrowed enough money from my parents to pay my next college tuition contract and repaid them from my wages.

As I worked, I also studied and wrote hundreds of letters to foundations seeking funding to continue attending school. I finally found two foundations willing to help me. Each foundation covered one tuition contract for me which was enough for me to graduate. I quit BSI as soon as I could afford it because I preferred studying and working with leather. I still made money with my hobby, just not as much as before. I had to cut lots of corners to get through school. I borrowed books from the interlibrary loan system when they were available to avoid having to buy them. I bought used books when I could find them and resold them as soon as the class was finished. As a last resort, I bought new texts and resold them after the class was over. It allowed me to use the same money over and over to pay for my textbooks. I graduated summa cum laude in December 1997 with a Bachelor of Science degree in Business

Administration with a major in marketing. I had a 3.95 GPA which qualified me for the Honor Roll.

After that, I went to work as a clerk for the community services director and kept that position until my transfer to Kettle Moraine Correctional Institution (KMCI).

But that isn't all I did at Fox Lake. Before I left Waupun, the PRC began mandating programs inmates must complete based on their offenses. Since I had a murder conviction I was required to take anger management. I had a very high opinion of myself. I thought I knew it all. Nobody could tell me anything. I had thought through every belief I had and determined that those beliefs were beyond question. If you didn't believe what I did, you were stupid and inferior. Arrogant was a term most people applied to me.

Funny thing about that anger management class I had to take. It was the start of a major metamorphosis in my worldview. One thing I knew about was self-defense. I had been defending myself my whole life and was currently serving a life sentence for defending myself against a much larger man. Self-defense came up in group and I opined that people have reflex actions that are beyond their control. Someone hits you, you automatically hit that person back. Cause and effect. Well, the counselor tried to explain it to me. Hitting a tendon on your knee and watching your leg jump was a reflex. Hitting someone back who hits you is a decision. Even though, by dint of constant repetition, the time that elapses between getting hit, the decision to hit back and the resulting action had become miniscule, it was still a conscious decision. I balked at this. It was one of my foundation beliefs. Unshakeable. My identity was tied very tightly to this belief.

Well, I pondered and meditated, thought long and hard. Finally, I had an epiphany. I was wrong! It was a choice I had made long ago. If you attack me, I respond with my own attack. Always. No matter what. No hesitation or pause to consider the cost. Kill or be killed. Wow. I was flabbergasted. If I had that basic fundamental belief wrong, what else did I have wrong? That was the first real step toward changing my life. I began a search which is still going on to this day. The search will last for the rest of my life. A search for the truth. I started reading every book on self-help, spirituality and emotional healing I could find. I questioned every belief I had. I prayed, meditated and performed rituals. I belonged to the Wiccan/Pagan group and did ceremonial magick rituals during the special days: solstices, equinoxes, etc. I began to have dreams and visions which gave me healing and awareness.

In one dream, I met my brother and forgave him for all the harm he did to me and repented of causing his death. I let go of a terrible burden by doing so. In another dream, my crippled leg was peeled apart and put together again, whole, healed and refreshed. It did not cure the physical disability but it healed me of the trauma of the accident and years of suffering which followed.

One of the most important (or life-changing) spiritual events was what I call the Vision of Cause and Effect. It seeped into my consciousness while I was awake and alert. I saw and experienced myself trying to climb a fog-enshrouded mountain. I blundered along blindly, overcame one obstacle after another. I didn't know where I was going to, or coming from, or why. It was a long, grueling journey. Finally, I came out on a ledge on the other side of the mountain. The fog was all behind me and before me I saw a large valley with multitudes of paths and roads with forks in them. I saw each road I could take and that I was free to choose any road. When I came to a fork in the road, I could then choose whatever path I wanted. But each path I chose would give a specific result and the only way that result would occur is if I made the choice that would render that result. The things you do cause the things that happen to you. This was a paradigm-shifting experience for me. All my life I believed that there was fate, karma and luck which determined what happened to me. I believed I was just unlucky with all the bad, painful things which happened in my life. I could now see it was all my doing caused by the choices I made.

I may have been terrorized by a sadistic older brother but I chose to resort to violence as a response. I may have been attacked without provocation by Dick Endres but I chose to stab him. I also chose to be at that apartment at 3 A.M. and to lead a lifestyle which would put me in harm's way. The choices I made got me the results I was facing today, tomorrow and for the rest of my life.

I guess the phrase "better late than never" applies here. I was in my 40s before I had this vision. From that point forward every action or decision in my life has been based on the outcome I want and what I think will increase the likelihood of that outcome occurring. Often, I have been conflicted over what would give me the desired result and chose as best I could. And when I was in a situation from which I could see no favorable outcome, I turned to my Holy Guardian Angel and put my fate in God's hands.

I joined the Self Help Group to learn to listen to other people and value the opinions and input of others. I joined Narcotics Anonymous and Alcoholics Anonymous to see what wisdom those groups had to offer. I met and fell in love with a wonderful woman just as I was experiencing all these changes in who I was as a person. Trish used to date a friend of mine and came to see me with him a couple of times. After they broke up, she came to see me and it was like I was struck by a lightning bolt. I fell in love with her immediately. I wrote her page after page of love letters telling of my beliefs, my spiritual path and what I wanted in a woman. She seemed to be the perfect mate for me. We courted in the visiting room and wed in the round chapel in Fox Lake, saying our own vows to each other. It was wonderful. I healed my emotions and let them have free rein to love her to the "depth and breadth and height my soul could reach" (Letters From the Portuguese, Elizabeth Barrett Browning). I made a lot of progress but, unknown to me, I still had a long way to go.

In May 2000, I was shanghaied out of Fox Lake and sent to Kettle Moraine because of some letters I sent to the warden criticizing the deputy warden. My world was shattered. I was angry and hurt. Kettle Moraine was a hell hole by comparison to Fox Lake. The staff were rude and unpleasant, the rules were restrictive and arbitrary and I was too far from my wife for regular visits. I became bitter. How could this happen to me? I filed a lawsuit against the deputy warden and railed against the injustice. I could see no way that good could come of my transfer. I again reacted by attacking when I was attacked. I wrote letters, filed grievances, and initiated lawsuits. I became despondent. I decided that I had had enough pain and suffering in my life. I would rather be dead than suffer any longer I no longer wanted to live. But how to die? I could not take my own life and be a mere suicide statistic. My death would have to have meaning. I decided that a hunger strike would be the best way to go. I found case law stating that force-feeding someone was a medical procedure and that I had a constitutional right to refuse medical treatment. So that was the plan. I told no one. I wanted to be sure because once I started out on this path there would be no turning back. I decided to give my spiritual path one last chance. I would do the supreme ritual of my belief system: Liber Samekh. If that was unsuccessful then I would go on a hunger strike and refuse to eat until I was freed from this bogus murder conviction. Liber Samekh is a six-month long ritual which is performed on the astral plane. I faithfully performed it as best as I could under the circumstances and, amazingly, it had a profound effect on me. I died after all. But not physically. I died to who I was and was reborn as a servant of God. Not my Will be done but Thine. It did not matter where I was but rather who I am as a person every day of my life. I saw the parole commission while at Kettle Moraine expecting nothing good and knowing that the outcome really didn't matter. I gave it all to my Holy Guardian Angel. I was blessed with an 11 month defer and a recommendation for work release. Praise God for his mercy. But cause and effect stepped in again. I had so angered everyone at Kettle Moraine that the PRC refused to transfer me to minimum security. Meanwhile, I was coming up on a jury trial for the retaliatory transfer to Kettle Moraine. I notified the court that I was now eligible for transfer to minimum security and that I would dismiss the lawsuit if I was transferred. The Classification Chief was one of the defendants in the action and also the person to decide whether I could transfer. He approved me to go to Oakhill and I dismissed the lawsuit.

I arrived at Oakhill in March 2002. After I transferred, I felt my spiritual state of bliss fading. My ego was reasserting itself and I had no opportunity do the rituals and meditations I needed to maintain my spiritual state. I wrote out a short manual of what I did to achieve my state before I lost the feeling of what it was. I expected to only spend a short while at Oakhill before I move on to a center, get work release and be paroled. But I got a surprise. Four months after I arrived at Oakhill, I received a new parole decision in the mail increasing my 11 month defer to a 24 month defer. I was aghast! How could she (the current parole commission chairperson, Diedre Morgan)? I felt all my plans fade away from me. I was pretty sure of what caused it but I had no proof. Oakhill was only ten miles from Madison and several staff members knew me or knew of me before I went to prison. More importantly, at least one of them had been a friend of Dick Endres. I suspect they contacted the parole commission about my favorable defer and endorsement for work release. Chairperson Morgan, never one to exercise compassion or restraint, responded with a scathing amended decision. My wife was crushed. It was the last straw for her. She seemed to give up hope at that point. It was a tense time for me. I asked my daughter, Santina, to come to see me in case I got sent back to medium and could not see her again for an untold number of years. I was so thankful she came and brought my two grandsons whom I had never seen before. However, not all of the Oakhill staff were against me. The PRC had to review my placement there and concluded that I should stay at Oakhill in spite of the new, increased defer.

It took me six months to overturn the 24 month defer via court action - from July 2002 until January 2003. Chairperson Morgan rescinded her decision and reinstated the 11 month defer to make the court action moot. But she wanted to leave the rescinded 24 month defer in my file "for record-keeping purposes." I argued against it in court alleging that it would be used against me at future parole and PRC hearings. The judge denied my request to delete it from my file.

By that time the 11 months of the defer had elapsed so I had another hearing with a different parole commission member who gave me a second 11 month defer. Chairperson Morgan amended that defer to a "no action" and referred it to the full commission for a decision. It appeared that she knew the administrative code as well as I did. She knew that the only time she could make a final decision on the length of my defer was if the case was referred to the full commission for a decision. Then they would make a recommendation to her which she could accept or change to whatever she wanted. I was prepared for her latest action. The administrative code also required that the matter be referred to the full committee by the commission member who conducted the hearing, not the chairperson. I expected Ms. Morgan to reject the committee's recommendation no matter what it was and give me another 24 month defer. However, a week after she referred my case to the full commission she was replaced as head of the parole commission. Lenard Wells took over and accepted the recommendation of the commission to give me another 11 month defer.

I thought I was on my way again after a short delay. I got another surprise from the PRC. They refused to give me an early hearing to send me to a work release center (they gave me an early hearing when my 11 month defer was changed to a 24). Then, at my regular hearing, they refused to accept the recommendation for work release made by the parole commission in January 2002 because it was not repeated in the subsequent parole decision. What was unstated but very clear by their actions was that the "rescinded" 24 month defer carried great weight and kept me from getting a transfer. The PRC would not let me transfer nor would the warden let me outside of the prison fence to work. Under the administrative code, I was permitted to leave the prison under escort by a staff member to work at an institution job. My boss at Badger State Industries tried several times to get me approved to no avail. I filed two court actions challenging these denials. These were certiorari actions where the court obtains the record upon which the administrative decision was made and reviews it for legality. Both trial courts were unreceptive to my claims. But the respective records showed that the classification chief and warden both relied on the 24 month defer to deny me what I asked for even after I was told that it would not be used against me.

Test My Mettle

Go ahead, test my mettle.
Make it as bad as you want.
Lock me in prison for a quarter century,
Don't let me see my daughter for a decade,
Make me scrape dirty dishes, eat crappy food,
Tease me, let me taste freedom,
Then take it away again.
Show me a light at the end of the tunnel,
Then reveal it's an oncoming train.
Doesn't matter, can't touch me.
Nothing you can do can take my joy,
Mar my mirth,
Extinguish my exuberance.
God gave me His grace,
When I gave him my life,
And you can never take my joy again.
May 11, 2010

I went back to the previous court where I had overturned the 24 month defer and sought once again to have the defer expunged from my record. I relied on the documents filed in the certiorari actions to prove that the court had been deceived when Chairperson Morgan told the court that the defer would not be used against me. The trial court denied me relief and I went to the court of appeals.

Meanwhile, I saw the parole commission again and again asking that the endorsement for work release be repeated so I could transfer. Each time, I was told that one endorsement from them was enough and it would not be repeated. The PRC, on the other hand, kept telling me that they would not transfer me unless I got another endorsement for work release from the parole commission. I was in limbo and could see no way to get any relief. I knew that everything happens for a reason but I couldn't see why I had to stay at Oakhill. What was the Holy Spirit keeping me there for? I finally found out.

I made it a point to take advantage of every program available to me. The only option when I first arrived at Oakhill was a course called No Free Lunch presented by Dr. Althouse of Clinical Services. I gained much valuable information about fiscal responsibility, living within my means and acquiring wealth. Eventually, other programs were offered that I was able to take such as Parenting and Prerelease Planning. I also did volunteer work crocheting items for homeless people and helping to run the Children's Video Project (guys could read books to their children on video and send the videos to the children). I sent many videos to my grandchildren. All of this was good for me. I learned a lot and came to a better understanding of myself and my interactions with my daughter, Santina, and grandsons, Ethan and Zander. However, it was the last program in which I participated that demonstrated to me once again that I was following a path laid out for me by the Holy Spirit.

Get the Edge came to Oakhill. They had a pep rally of sorts in the gym to generate interest and then they offered a ten-week course for a dozen or so guys. I was not chosen and of those who were chosen, several backed out at the last minute. Some replacements were hurriedly recruited and the program went ahead. A friend of mine made it into the first course and was able to recommend me for inclusion when the course was offered a second time.

Cay was a volunteer who had been running this course in Taycheedah Correctional Institution (Wisconsin's primary women's prison) for quite a while. She came to Oakhill to offer it there as well. She had participated in many of Tony Robbins seminars and was teaching us as part of his nonprofit foundation outreach to disadvantaged people who couldn't afford his seminars. Now I don't know about most people but I'm not a very gullible or trusting person. I had never heard of Tony Robbins before and he struck me as a bit of a snake oil salesman. The kind of person who sells you the sizzle to get you to buy the steak. Even though I was skeptical, I resolved that I would attend this course faithfully with an open mind and glean whatever wisdom I could from the teachings. I had been reading books on self-improvement and spirituality every chance I got. When the group started, I read Tony's books and also ordered all the books he referred to in his books so I could read them as well. I expected another intellectual exercise from the class, doing what I was taught and seeing if I could learn from it. My first impression of Cay was that she was smooth, too smooth, too sincere, in short, too good to be true. I really didn't trust her and even recorded that observation in my meditation journal. But I kept an open mind and vowed to do whatever was required of me in the program. One aspect of the program was what Cay referred to as one-on-one coaching sessions. She never really explained what they were, just asked the class each week who wanted one that week. I volunteered one week just to see what would happen. At our meeting she asked me what problem I had or issue I wanted to address. I had done so much spiritual work through meditation, prayer and ritual that I was not aware that I had any sort of thought patterns or personality issues she could help me with. I had adopted the Buddhist belief that "all is sorrow" which for me means that all of one's ego-centered desires are the cause of all the sorrow in one's life. I had given up on ever having a happy or joyous life. I merely trudged along my spiritual path doing God's will.

I told her that for me being told "no" equaled rejection and that I felt it in my heart every time I was told "no". Cay led me on the most amazing guided visualization I had ever experienced in my life. I had held the hurt and pain of 20 years of wrongful incarceration in my heart believing that I would never rest, never relax, never feel peace until I was vindicated for the murder for which I received a life sentence. Cay helped me release all that bound up energy and let go of those beliefs. I couldn't believe the change in me. I felt like I was high on cocaine for days afterward. I had more energy than the energizer bunny on TV commercials. I came away from that one session a healed and whole person.

What did she do to me? How did she do that? Was it something special that I was able to experience because I had prepared myself through my previous spiritual practices or could anyone get the same results? I had to learn more. I eventually learned the technique variously called neuro-linguistic programming, neuro-associative conditioning or core transformation. From that day forward I became Cay's staunchest supporter and advocate. As the course progressed, I was able to have additional one-on-one sessions with her. They were all good but none matched the first breakthrough I had with Cay. At the next course I volunteered to help her and ran the CD portion of the course for her.

I could probably go on and on about all of Cay's virtues but it would not serve any purpose. Let me merely say that Cay is one of the most extraordinary women I've ever met. She not only talks the talk, she walks the walk. I've encountered many people who know what they should be doing with their lives but never aspire to meet those goals. Cay is on a search for perfection in herself. She sets higher and higher goals and expectations for herself and meets them. My definition of following a spiritual path is to constantly seek to perfect oneself to the best of one's knowledge and ability. The closer one approaches to perfection, the closer one comes to God. Cay is consciously on a path to reach the greatest possible state of achievement she can. I doubt if she views it as I do, i.e., that to seek perfection in oneself is to follow a spiritual path. But it most assuredly is what she is doing.

I found out later that not all people are equally receptive to the guided meditation I received from Cay. Many people are too afraid to open themselves up in that manner. Some are just not ready yet. I was blessed in getting such a wonderful outcome from my efforts. It is the reason the Holy Spirit kept me at Oakhill for all those years.

I finally got a decision back on my appeal about leaving the 24 month defer in my file. The appellate court agreed with me that the 24 month defer had been used against me and remanded the action back to the trial court for relief. There were no objections this time. The prejudicial documents were removed from my file. At my next PRC hearing I was recommended for transfer to a center with community custody so I could go on work release. While I was waiting for a final decision from the classification chief on a transfer, I had another parole hearing where I was given a ten month defer and another endorsement for work release. After almost 4 years at Oakhill, I was transferred to Gordon Correctional Center. The trip to get there was quite an experience.

It all began on Dec. 9, 2005, at about 12:45 p.m. I loaded my 4 boxes of property and my keyboard on the bus. After being divested of my coat, hat and gloves and a cursory pat search, I entered the DOC transport bus. I was thankful for the expansive windows so I could view the sights as we drove along (one of the buses has all of its windows covered with metal sheets). I marveled at, and luxuriated in, the fact that I was the ONLY passenger in that large bus., The seats were hard, molded fiberglass which became uncomfortable after a while but not exceedingly so as I was too engrossed in sight-seeing to pay much notice.

We arrived in style at DCI and I disembarked with a light heart and a bounce in my step. My property was stacked up and in I went to wait in a holding tank with a diverse group of men who had arrived just ahead of me. After some delay (and a late bag lunch) we were strip searched. Lunch was 2 sandwiches (one baloney and one cheese), carrots, milk, raisins and a cookie (I traded my baloney for cheese and my cookie for carrots and raisins). We were then given another identical bag supper and led off to the infamous dungeon - unit 17 - to be housed in the narrow, cold transfer corridor.

There are 7 transfer cells located in an obscure hallway partially beneath ground level. Each cell had 3 bunks. Once we are in, we are there until we transfer out. We can get a shower 3 days after arrival although we all hoped we would not be there that long. I was placed with 2 men, one of whom had been left there an extra week for some unknown reason. Maybe they just forgot him last week. Usually, men pass through in less than 7 days. I was there from Friday to the next Tuesday. The other guy, Terry, was coming back from 90 days of warehousing in a northern county jail.

The cells had not been cleaned in months, maybe even years, and despite our requests we were not allowed to do any cleaning. The cell I was in was so cold that I had to exercise several hours a day to get warm enough to crawl under the one thin blanket they provided and try to get some sleep on the rock-hard mattress. If I slept on my back, my kidneys would hurt; if I slept on my side, my hips would hurt. I had no pillow -I used a stack of old magazines which was surprisingly comfortable.

My cell mates were mellow, easy-going guys and I enjoyed interacting with them. When we first entered, we were each warned to keep our one disposable plastic spoon because we would not get another one. I told the others that it was because they were magic spoons and everything we ate with them would taste good. Soon, they joined me in the magic spoon merriment which delighted us all. For the first 3 days I slept very little. I was so excited to be on my way. And it was too cold to sleep. I'd end up shivering under my blanket even though I had a thermal top and a long sleeve shirt. On the 3rd day Cory discovered that the security window was not tightly closed because Terry had fiddled with it the first day and left it open. It warmed up a few degrees after that and it was just enough so I could sleep a little bit more on the final night.

On Tuesday, the long timer, Cory, and I left Terry behind and headed off to our destinations. Stripped again and this time my wrists were cuffed with a chain belt and a black box (the black box fits over the cuffs to immobilize them which makes them very uncomfortable, especially for fat people, and prevents the possibility of opening the cuffs). I was riding with guys rated medium and maximum security so we all had to be cuffed. We lucked out and got another windowed bus. Not only that, the seats were padded! Glory be! What a pleasure that was. Much softer than the rock-hard mattress I had just spent 4 days on.

We rolled out and stopped at Waupun for a pick up. As we waited, I watched 2 female prisoners from John Burke Center as they went about their morning cleaning routine at the front gate. Inmates from within Waupun prison are not allowed outside of the walls so women from the nearby minimum facility clean up out in front of the prison. Next stop was Fox Lake for another pick up. I had spent 7 years there in the 90s and even though there were now many more fences in the compound I still remembered it as a positive place in which to grow and change. We went to Columbia Correctional Institution near Portage next. Somehow the driver managed to find a route that took him through downtown Wisconsin Dells which was a treat for me. I hadn't been there in over 20 years (since before I came to prison). So many new tourist traps. So many old familiar sights. I kept an eagle eye out for potential sights to sell the products from my future business. I noted one house on main street that appealed to me. We finally got to Columbia and left some guys behind. We took the interstate from there. As we passed the Mauston exit I thought of my aunt Lucille. New Lisbon prison was an oppressive looking place, but then, aren't almost all prisons? We dropped some off and added some. Next stop, Jackson.

I remembered some unique familiar rock formations along the interstate. Soon, we rolled into my new temporary home. I thought I was going to a minimum barracks. HA! First, it was a strip search again. The guards had a fit because I had on special shoes as well as a comb and eye glasses. They took my ID tag only to give it back later with a thick rough necklace to wear it on. I much preferred my light, plastic one. Oh well, when in Rome . . .

We went to the barracks. It was set up essentially like all the other barracks I had been to. The only difference was the multitude of rules of such bizarre, unwarranted nature that they could only exist to give the staff a pretext to harass inmates. Actually, I should say the rules probably exist to give the staff something to do. That is a much more charitable view than to believe the rules are only intended as tools of harassment. Let me cite some examples.

We could not stand up - either outside or in the dayroom. We cannot walk away from our bunk and leave anything on the bunk nor could we leave our property drawer unlocked. And we could not hang anything off the end of our beds.

These rules were zealously enforced. Also, we could not wear our winter coats inside, not even to put them on to walk outside. We had to wait until we were outside to put our winter coats on. On the other hand, we could wear our summer coats anywhere and everywhere. At meals we could wear whatever we wanted as well. There was a washer and dryer but we had to buy laundry tokens to use them and we had to wait until our money arrived in our accounts to buy the tokens and that usually takes several weeks.

I gave up my good greens and got mental institution clothes. I call them that because there is only one pocket on the pants (a back pocket) and they have elastic waistbands so we don't need belts but they always fit loosely and have a tendency to fall down when we try to do anything strenuous. Just right for a guy in a mental institution so doped up he can't do anything but lay around in a stupor and drool. For anyone else, they are a great inconvenience. I didn't like the clothes but it really doesn't matter because I'm going home soon. Recreation is another bizarre experience. We have to wear the institution's shorts and t-shirts and must carry our own shoes (if we have them, or else they provide shoes) and put them on after changing our clothes. I did get a good haircut (relatively speaking) and compared to where I've been the canteen is fantastic. I planned on spending $100 or more to stock up on things I'll need before I move on to a center.

I had a realization while at Jackson. A NEVER AGAIN moment. I will never come back to prison again in my life (yes, this is my second time, I didn't learn anything the first time). After experiencing the hostility and ill treatment which permeates this place I know I will not return to prison under any circumstances. I refuse to ever put myself in a position where I will be treated like this again. I'm going to get out, start my businesses, amass wealth and make political connections and insulate myself from any further abuse by the criminal justice system. It's a shame I had to spend decades in prison to get a lick of sense. Better late than never.

(continued at Gordon Correctional Center on December 22, 2005).

On Tuesday, Dec. 20th I got my account statement and was looking forward to ordering canteen. Alas, it was not to be. Much to my surprise and relief, I was told to pack up to leave the next day. And so I did. I got some of my mail right after that so I had to carry it with me on the trip. Tuesday, 8 days after arrival, off we went in a van with a trailer attached. I hoped my keyboard was there. We had to get shackles and leg chains because 2 guys going to Stanley prison were TLU status (temporary lock up pending a conduct report). No strip searches, just pat downs.

We took the back roads and I have no idea what roads we took or how we got there but I loved the scenery. For all I know, there are nothing but back roads this far north. Stanley is said to be an unpleasant place and from what little I saw, it was. We stopped long enough to drop off the TLU guys and add to our group -

all minimum security so no chains. But the 11 of us were quite crowded and my spot on the van was very cold.

We went to Flambeau Center and there we changed vehicles. We ate lunch in their dining room. I saw several guys I knew and a staff member I recognized from my days in Waupun. The feeling I got was one of hostility by the staff towards the inmates and I was glad I would not be staying there. The guys I knew were Kurt Kethley, Terry Erickson and Kevin Kmecik. Gordon and McNaughton Centers sent their own vehicles to pick up new guys and drop off guys heading south. Another guy and I got in the car headed to Gordon. I noticed my key board did not make it on the trip with me. We drove past the lodge with the huge black bear statue out front where I once stayed during a fishing trip back in the early 80s. We drove all the back roads and it was wonderful. Many small towns along the way. Phenomenal.

Gordon Work Release Center

I was pleasantly surprised when I arrived at Gordon Correctional Center in December 2005. Compared to the previous years spent inside one prison after another, it was heaven. On the other hand, it was one of the more restrictive work release centers – needlessly so in my opinion. Nevertheless, I worked at institution jobs until my turn came up for work release.

Arriving there was a profound relief. The food tastes great (they could do with some pointers on nutrition), the staff are great and the living conditions are ok. There are a couple of minor glitches but they don't really matter at this time. The 3rd shift officer sorted through our property while we slept and gave it to us at 5:30 a.m. the next morning. I had to give up the hood from my personal winter coat (because it was detachable), my surge protector and some photos - no big deal. As soon as my money is transferred I will order thermal underwear, typewriter cartridges and new shoes. As I sit here penning these final words, I am washing my clothes. They have high tech, state of the art washers and dryers.

I didn't mind the petty rules and inconveniences because I KNEW that I was finally on my way home. I assumed that I'd go on work release for a while, get a prerelease plan request from the parole commission and most likely be released within a year. However, it didn't turn out that way.

The center was located along the Eau Claire River, in Douglas County. The river at that point wasn't much more than a small creek, mostly only a few feet deep and varying in width from 15 to 45 feet. It was deep enough, however, for fish to survive and prisoners were allowed to go fishing. Catch and release only. Some guys caught muskies and northern pikes of fairly good size. They even had 3 row boats so the guys could go out into the one largish bay where the water was deeper and where the big fish dwelled. I never did any fishing there. I had planned to but the superintendent suspended access to the river right after I arrived for some silly reason – probably because some of the guys were smoking while fishing (the river was mostly out of sight of the buildings and surveillance cameras) – so I decided not to waste my time and money buying fishing gear that I may never be able to use and may have to dispose of at some point. Additionally, although the northern centers all had fishing privileges, most of the southern centers didn't and I was determined to get to a southern center,

Gordon was located about 100 yards from the Eau Claire River and we were allowed to walk around a fairly large area, including alongside the river. I spent many hours sitting there, listening to the water flow by and soaking up the wonderful healing natural beauty all around me. I loved to walk down to the river to sit and meditate while listening to the relaxing sound of the river flowing over the rocks. I bided my time, slowly got used to being treated more like a human than I had been for years. There were no clocks there so I had to buy a watch just to make sure that I didn't stay by the river too long and miss one of the mandatory counts, of which there were several per day. I felt all the strain and tension of decades in prison melt away as I became one with nature. It made me feel healed and whole. It recharged my emotional and spiritual batteries as I sat there meditating. The staff had apparently never had a prisoner who meditated because they often made their rounds and stopped to check on me, sure I was doing something I wasn't supposed to, but never figuring out what it was. Eventually, they came to realize that I was just different from the other prisoners. I worked at an institution job for a while as a laundry worker. I washed all the state clothes, sheets, towels, etc., for a few months before I was allowed to go on work release. I then spent 19 months working at Jack Links Beef Jerky in Minong, Wisconsin. It was cold, unpleasant work but compared to prison wages, it was fabulous. Every time I saw the prison classification committee, I requested transfer to a southern work release center where I would have more (and better) opportunities for work release. Finally, after 19 months of work release, they recommended me and I was approved for transfer.

For Whom the Bell Tolls

The bell rings and rings
'Til you think the button is stuck,
Sounding like the recess bell in
My grade school decades past,
Waking up the camp for another day.
The Jack Links workers coming back,
Dog-tired, smelling of cooked meat,
Sickly sweet, greasy, like a cold
Skillet after cooking bacon and eggs.
There is no excuse here for missing breakfast,
One of the first formal counts of the day.
To a man who's never known shackles,
Or the mighty oppression of his government
This would be a hellhole beyond compare.
Less fortunate citizens, having been
Intimate with too many state prisons for
Too many years, are grateful for that
Miserable bell, the bell of freedom
Meaning no more shackles, locked cells,
Or blue shirts saying have a nice day
And meaning the opposite.
Good food, humane treatment, nestled in the
Eau Claire River Valley, so long in prison

It's hard to imagine that life can
Get better than this out in the
Free World, where choices are made,
Dreams are fulfilled, happiness found.
To think that there is really more
To life than cessation of pain,
That a comfortable pair of shoes feels better
Than the urge of relief after removing
The pebble you walked on for so long.
So grateful just not to hurt any more,
No longer able to imagine what that new
Pair of shoes would feel like,
August 26, 2010

So there I was in a work release center with the most freedom I had enjoyed in decades. Until transferring to Gordon Correctional Center, I had to wear shackles every time I went out in public. Not anymore. I could wear all my own clothes everywhere except when I left the facility. I started out in a hallway where overflow new arrivals were housed. I stayed there for a couple of weeks until I got a job in the institution laundry which entitled me to move to a four-man room. My roommates were pretty good guys. There was a lot of turnover and movement via transfers in and out but it didn't seem to matter. Unlike higher security facilities there weren't any of the usual problem prisoners. For the most part, nobody had a bad attitude or went out of their way to make life difficult for the other prisoners. I think there are two reasons for this. Generally, the more well-behaved prisoners were approved to go to a work release center and the stress and unpleasantness of higher security which drove many men to act up was gone. When the onerous conditions went so did the bad behavior. The main work release site for Gordon was Jack Link's Beef Jerky and on some of the jobs the guys got bloody working with raw meat or working on third shift cleaning up after the bloody mess. All the bloody clothes were washed in the institution laundry. I also washed kitchen rags and the state-issued clothing and bedding used by the other prisoners. It was at Gordon that I decided to write this Memoir. I finally had access to a computer where I could type whatever I wanted so I wrote out my Memoir by hand and every time the computer lab was open, I transcribed my notes. I also typed up many of my poems and stored them in the computer. The DOC had a large server for prisoners who were given computer access where they could save their documents. At higher security we could only store school assignments and other authorized documents but at work release centers we could create anything we wanted and save it. We could also purchase floppy disks - the current technology at the time - to save our writings.

When I arrived at Gordon Correctional Center for the first time, I knew I was on my way home. The only way I could be sent back to a higher security facility and kept longer was if I did something wrong – which I was determined not to do. I had heard so many stories and seen so many people get sent back to higher security for doing stupid things I was amply warned about what not to do. In my eyes, it was just a waiting game. Sooner or later, I would be paroled. I knew that I had to go on work release which I was finally eligible to do.

I had talked about writing a book for years. I even promised my Higher Power that I would do so. But I could not seem to be able to motivate myself to do it. I finally got started at Gordon Correctional Center. I arrived there and had to live in a hallway for 3 weeks which I pompously called an "alcove" before I went into a 4-man room. I was put to work in the center laundry and worked as hard as I could. I fretted that I would not get work release for months because there were so few jobs. I gave it to God to handle for me. Meanwhile, I talked to many guys there and they often said things that did not ring true. I would counter with an observation or point of view which was based on my past learning and experiences and had never occurred to them before. After all the time I spent changing myself these things were a part of me. For others, it was new territory. It became noteworthy among my roommates because I spoke most often with them. Each time I came out with one of my insights they would point it out and tell me I should put it down in a book. They helped me coin the phrase "Harlanisms" to give a name to my comments.

The Holy Grail of many prisoners who arrive at a minimum-security center is to get a driver's license. I, too, wanted to get my license when I finally arrived at a work release center but it proved much harder than I ever imagined. I often counseled myself with that adage used by Tony Robbins: God's delays are not God's denials.

When I arrived at Gordon Correctional Center I learned that a month earlier the warden over the entire camp system issued an order that prisoners would no longer be allowed to use state

146

vehicles to practice for or take their road test. Since the last time I drove had been over 21 years ago, I knew I needed to take both the written and road tests.

My "can do" attitude kicked in and I resolved to overcome whatever hurdles I faced to get my license. Kirk, the staff member in charge of helping prisoners get a drivers license was on a sabbatical when I arrived so I had to wait for him to return to work. He gave me the bad news about the road tests (which I had already heard) the first time I talked to him. Nevertheless, I insisted on taking the written test figuring that I would find a way to get the road test after that. I ordered the check to pay the fee in February and waited for my trip to the Department of Motor Vehicles (DMV).

The superintendent at that time had no interest in addressing the issue so I had hoped to get a transfer to another center before the instruction permit expired. But nothing ever stays the same and we were blessed with a new superintendent who had her own set of priorities about how to run a center.

I continued to wait for my chance to take my written test knowing the delay would not hurt me in fulfilling my plan. The clock only started running after I got the permit and I had one year to get a transfer and take my road test. At the end of July, on a beautiful sunny day, I was taken to Hayward DMV to take my test. It was 7 months after I arrived and 4 months after I had ordered the check to pay the fee. I had heard that all DMV tests were now on computer but at Hayward they were still using written tests. I assume that this was because Hayward was a parttime office that was only open one day per week. I got a perfect score on the test.

I wrote to the superintendent suggesting that she make a deal with the local high school driver's education teacher to take prisoners for their road tests. She did not respond to my letter but she did make arrangements with a driving school in Superior to provide instruction and a vehicle for our tests. She turned the matter over to Kirk to finalize.

I began to stop in to see Kirk regularly to get my road test set up. He was in charge of the school and library, taught Cognitive Growth Intervention Program (CGIP) classes and had many other duties as well. I ordered the check to pay for the road test in August but had no idea how much I would have to pay the driving school to use their vehicle. By October, Kirk got the information from the driving school and I ordered the check. When that check arrived in November, Kirk scheduled an appointment with the DMV for the road test. It was in January, two months away and 13 months after I arrived at Gordon.

I waited impatiently for the scheduled day. I had big plans. The camp system uses prisoners to drive their vans to take other prisoners to work release sites and I wanted to get certified to do that. But during my long ordeal another new policy was issued regarding van drivers. They now had to have two years of documented driving experience in order to become "van certified" to drive the prison vans. I found out when I took my written test that the Wisconsin DMV expunges all driving records 8 years, 6 months after a license has expired. Even though I had 15 years of prior driving experience, officially I had none. I did not exist in the DMV database.

Hoping that there were some old DMV files still in existence, I wrote to the DMV office in Madison asking about their old records. No such luck. No old files. They keep records of drunk driving convictions forever but those of us with good driving records get erased. I also wrote to the Illinois DMV because I previously held an Illinois license when I lived in that state. I did not hear back from them for months and concluded that they threw my inquiry away when they found they had no such records of my license. I then planned to ask the driving instructor from the school to give me a written evaluation of my driving skills when she took me for my road test so I could submit it when I sought van certification.

The fateful day neared. I was ready. There wasn't much work at the factory where I was employed so I already had the day off. I went over to talk to Kirk the day before the test to make sure everything was ready. He had bad news for me. There was a scheduling conflict and the driving school instructor was not available to take me to the test. Apparently, she did not get the email notifying her of the test and had a prior commitment. We had to reschedule. I got a new date for the following month which was confirmed in advance by all parties so there would be no other cancellations. I had to wait some more. Remember, God's delays are not God's denials.

Later that day, during mail call, I got a response from the Illinois DMV. What a surprise! They verified my driver's license from

Illinois in writing. Now I could prove I had a driver's license, get a regular driver's license and become van certified.

February 16th, my scheduled day, was here at last. Fourteen months after I arrived at Gordon I was finally ready to get my license. At 8:00 a.m. I went to the officer's station and asked if I could go over to the school to talk to Kirk so I could find out what time we were leaving. I was told he was not here. What? Again? Surely not! I showed them my appointment sheet and they said there was no release order to allow me to make the trip. They asked me if Kirk knew about it. Of course he knew, he gave me the appointment slip! But as we spoke they checked the date book and saw that Kirk was penciled in for an 8:00 a.m. arrival. I looked out the window and saw him driving up. Whew! That was a close one.

Then the sergeant told me that I had to change my clothes and put on a prison uniform to take my test. I had anticipated this and earlier in the week wrote to the superintendent to ask her if I could wear my own clothes when I went to take the test. She replied in writing in the affirmative. I showed the officers the note and settled the matter.

Kirk grabbed my checks from the safe and my instruction permit and social security card from my property file and away we went. I made sure to listen to the weather report for the day. It was clear, with only a 20% chance of snow in the afternoon. My test would be over before the snow arrived. As we motored north, Kirk gave me a few pointers about driving and we discussed some traffic laws so I could get clarification. It was about a 45-minute drive.

About ten miles from Superior, snow flurries began. Uh-oh. It can't be snowing! I can't get the test canceled because of bad weather! Further south, in Madison, there is a good chance that snow would cause all appointments to be canceled. Kirk, however, assured me that a little snow would not interfere with the scheduled road test.

We found the driving school, met the instructor and Kirk left us to go on by ourselves. Darlene, the driving instructor, had a cute little Buick with the most wonderful amenities: Power everything, adjustable steering wheel, individual temperature controls, automatic headlights, remote starter, backup warning sensor, the works. For me it was like climbing into the cockpit of a spaceship. It was so different from the last vehicle I drove - a 1968 Chevy van.

I practiced driving for an hour. I parallel parked, Y-turned, backed up, went forward, crossed roads, turned left and right. I did everything well. No problems. Except for the snow. It kept coming down harder and harder. The wind was blowing as well. I wondered if this was one of those Lake Superior "lake effect" storms that would dump a couple of feet of snow on the ground. We went to the DVM office and I registered. I waited only 5 or 10 minutes for my test.

The DMV examiner called me and we went outside. The car had already snowed up. The windows were covered. I had to start the engine and get the scraper out of the trunk to clean the windows. He checked all the lights, the horn, the wipers and the emergency brake. We started out and there was already at least an inch of snow on the ground and more steadily falling. The interesting part was that when we first arrived in Superior, I could see that there was no old snow on the ground at all - strange for being so far north in February. It seemed liked the snow chose to come just to challenge me on my road test.

I stopped, I started, Y-turned, backed up, went forward, parked - everything he asked me to do. I did it all perfectly and returned to the DMV. He gave me the test results: A perfect score. In spite of the snow and not having driven for over 22 years, I completed my test and earned my license.

I presented my letter from Illinois to the clerk and asked for a regular license because I had previously held a license. But, upon review, the supervisor stated that since it was more than 8 years, 6 months ago I had to start over with a probationary license. Oh well, at least I have a license. Then the clerk looked at my check and saw that it was only good for 180 days and that it had been issued last August. She started counting the days. It was the 179th day and she had to talk to her supervisor about whether to accept the check. He said okay and I assured them that I would send another one if that one was rejected. Whew!

I eventually got to go to work at Jack Links. Such a blessing to earn a real working wage pay where I could pay into Social Security while also getting a glimpse of the Free World. Gordon was a northern Work Release Center where there weren't many Work Release jobs available. I kept requesting transfer to a southern Work Release Center where I could get a better job. Jack Link's was cold, hard work where I had to stand for 8 hours per day in a refrigerated room. My old motorcycle injury was getting worse as I got older – stiffer, more painful, less movement. It made working there very difficult but I knew that I had to be on work release to get parole. About this time a new parole commission member named Danielle Lacost came to Gordon to hold hearings. My hearing with her did not go well. She was outraged that I was out on work release with what she considered a short amount of time served in light of my prior manslaughter conviction and current murder conviction. She gave me a 10-month defer and I transferred to Sanger Powers shortly after that so I thought I wouldn't have to worry about her.

I wanted to get to a southern work release center because there were more job opportunities there and the Jack Links job I had caused me daily pain due to my crippled leg. The Program review Committee (PRC) approved me for transfer and in November 2007 I was transferred to Sangar Powers Correctional Center (SPCC). The differences between the two facilities were astounding. GCC was tightly controlled and any rule infractions were dealt with immediately. SPCC, on the other hand, was like the Wild West. Prisoners routinely ignored rules and weren't punished for their actions. Also, things were much more relaxed and there were less rules altogether. Another thing that SPCC had which wasn't available in GCC was their computer system in the library. There were 6 computers networked together that had video games on them. The prisoners could sign up for game time and play multiple-person games. What I thought was strange considering that it was part of the prison was that the superintendent permitted violent video games. There was a first-person shooter game that multiple prisoners could play at one time where they hunted each other down. Does it really make sense to allow a video game like that to be played by guys serving life sentences for murder? I was a van driver for 2 weeks at Sangar Powers when someone from the main office called the superintendent and told him to restrict me to the work release center. It was all coming together and not in a good way. The superintendent tried to persuade me to voluntarily return to Oakhill (which I refused to do) or take a maintenance job which I couldn't do because of my crippled leg. I ended up being a custodian and photographer. I also got involved in the dog program. They had an arrangement with the local Humane Society where they would take rescue dogs to the center and let them live with one of the prisoners for 90 days. The guys were expected to socialize the dogs and teach them basic commands so that they would be more desirable as adoptable pets. I helped train several dogs while I was there.

After I had been there about 6 months, I had a parole hearing with the same woman who gave me the first endorsement for work release 6 years earlier. It was like being reviewed by a different person. She gave me no action and referred my case to the full commission. They only do that when they are planning to change your status. Since I hadn't yet received a request for a pre-release investigation and I knew that they weren't planning to parole me it meant that they wanted to raise my defer. She was critical and hostile. I showed her this Memoir and explained how I planned to get out, get it published and use my life story to help guide others. She gave me a no action and referred my case to the full commission. I knew then that I was going to get a bad decision and when a "no action" is given it usually means that the commission member doesn't want to be the one to make the final decision - either because the person wanted to recommend parole or issue an adverse decision. Based on our interview I knew that it wasn't to release me on parole. Sure enough, a couple of months later the guards surrounded me, handcuffed me and took me to the segregation unit in Redgranite Correctional Institution. I had done nothing wrong! I had been on 19 months of work release and drove a van unsupervised throughout the Green Bay Area. But since my parole defer had been raised for no apparent reason from a 10 to a 12 month defer, I now became a security risk. At Redgranite I wrote the security director and explained my situation. The next day I was released from segregation into general population. I was given an emergency reclassification hearing and my custody level was increased to minimum from community custody. Other minimum security prisoners were permitted to stay at work release centers but not me. I was returned to Oakhill - a secure minimum - which is a euphemism for a prison with fewer rules than a medium security prison. I was back in Oakhill 8 days after being removed from Sanger Powers. I knew that the decision couldn't stand. There's a procedure for judicial review of administrative decisions called certiorari. Part of that review entails evaluating the decision to determine whether it was arbitrary and capricious and not supported by substantial evidence in the record. Nothing negative had occurred and there's no way that the court could find that it wasn't arbitrary and capricious. Yet it did. The court essentially held that it was irrelevant what prior decisions had been issued by the same administrative agency. Their judicial review merely looked at the record before the agency to determine whether any view of the record would support the decision. They held that a reasonable person could have reviewed the record and issue the increase defer so the courts upheld the decision. I challenged the transfer decision as well but also lost that case on essentially the same grounds. I tried to get back into Badger State Industries where I could make a $1.60 an hour - enough to live on and send some to my daughter to help her out - but the administration made it clear that they didn't want me to have a good-paying job with pleasant working conditions after returning to Oakhill. I ended up getting an institution job as a servery worker at one of the Cottages where I made less than 20 cents an hour. I needed to hold a job if I was going to have a chance of getting a reduced parole defer so I could return to a work release center.

While at Oakhill I learned about something called A Course in Miracles. I ordered a book and read about how two psychologists in the 1970s began receiving guided writings from a discarnate entity who claimed to be Jesus. They were impressed and inspired by the information passed on to them and were persuaded of the validity of the message. As I read the book, I also became persuaded of the truth of what was revealed. At the end of the book was a section containing 365 daily exercises. I resolved to do one a day until I completed them all. Meanwhile I served out my 12 month defer and then an 11-month defer. Finally, I was given a 10 month defer which once again made me eligible for community custody and transfer. I was reapproved for placement in a northern Work Release Center. A Course in

Miracles had convinced me that Jesus Christ was real. I bought a Bible and began studying it. I knew nothing about Christianity except that it was an evil thing but I was able to read the Bible with new eyes and began to understand that it wasn't Jesus or his message that was to blame. It was the people misinterpreting his message. I could go on and on about all the atrocities committed by Christians over the centuries in the name of the Lord but that's not what's important. From the first time he spoke to my heart, I have endeavored to do his will to the best of my ability. It all boils down to the two greatest commandments: to love God with all your heart and mind and soul and strength and to love your neighbor as yourself. I don't always know the best path to travel. I often doubt myself and I'm not sure what God's path for me is but I do the best I can and when I realize that I've been mistaken in something I admit it and resolved to do better. On the day I completed the 365th lesson in A Course in Miracles I was told to pack up for transfer. Once again I took the bus to DCI and then to Jackson Correctional Institution. Once again I was taken in a van to Flambeau Correctional Center where I was transferred to another van heading back to Gordon. I had hoped to end up in McNaughton but I guess since I did so well at Gordon the first time I was there I was slated to return. I started out as a reentry Clerk and eventually I was approved to be a van driver. I believed that I would continue to drive a van at Gordon until I was paroled. I loved driving, especially when I had to make trips to pick up the workers at Shell Lake an hour away from the center. I would leave at 2:00 a.m. and have an hour of solitude in the van listening to ethereal music. The only challenge was to watch for deer on the side of the road and there are a lot of them. You never knew when one would freak out over the oncoming headlights and dart out into the road. I developed a strategy of blowing my horn when I saw the reflection of my headlights in deer's eyes. The horn would prevent them from getting mesmerized by my headlights. I never hit a deer.

In the fall of 2010 I had my next parole hearing. Much to my dismay, Danielle Lacost held the hearing - the same one who got outraged over what I had to say the last time I had a hearing with her. She gave me a no action and I was pretty sure that her intention wasn't to seek my release on parole. I was hopeful that saner heads would prevail and that the chairman would give me a favorable decision in spite of Lacost's animosity towards me. The gubernatorial election was going on and I was hoping that a Democrat would be elected unfortunately Republican Scott Walker won the election. He was the assembly majority leader a decade earlier and was responsible for getting Truth In Sentencing (TIS) passed. He believed that even old-law prisoners with parole eligibility shouldn't be released early on parole. One week after his inauguration, the parole commission issued a decision increasing my defer back up to 12 months. I was disappointed, especially when they transferred me to Douglas County Jail pending an early reclassification hearing.

Douglas County Jail
I know I have spent worse nights,
Slept on harder beds, gotten less sleep
Than I did on my first night in
Douglas County Jail, but
I really can't remember where or when.

It must have been in my teen years
Where a bare floor was as good as
Anything and it didn't matter
Where or how I passed out
Before the next bout of drinking.
Except for a seg cell here or there,
Nothing in these last decades of prison
Have equaled the misery
I found in a too flat mattress
Under a too bright light.

January 8, 2011

THE SAGA CONTINUES

I expected to be sent back to Oakhill to wait for another more favorable decision. I got the surprise of my life when the decision came back to increase my custody level to medium and transfer me to the worst medium facility prison in the state: Stanley Correctional Institution. After 9 years of relative freedom and humane treatment, I was back in a real prison experiencing all that entailed. I was devastated, stuck in a two-man cell in a concrete and steel building with only 10 hours per day outside of the cell. I hated it. I hated the strip searches, the shackles, the callous treatment. I was lucky that a friend of mine from years earlier got me a job in the library when I first arrived which was a haven compared to the rest of the prison. The food was the worst I'd ever had in prison. During the 9 years I was at minimum facilities the conditions at mediums and maximums had gotten increasingly oppressive and restrictive and unpleasant. I struggled to adapt, eventually getting acclimated to the misery.

Sucked Down Into the Mire By a Bi-Polar Celly
Every morning I stand at the
Top of a slippery slope waiting to see
If my cellmate is going to slide down

160

Into the mire of his hateful bi-polar self or
Grab a handful of happy-helium balloons
To float into cloud nine-o-mania.
Each time I must choose whether
To follow him down the slide, float off
In heliumistic euphoria or stand
My ground, perhaps showing him
Once and for all that it doesn't have to
Be this way, that he can wake up
Each morning on an even keel,
Setting a course to a better life, and
Sail off into a glorious future.
November 25, 2012

I wondered how God could choose to punish me after I became a Christian. It made no sense but I resolved that I wouldn't let it shake my newfound faith. I attended the church services, studied the Bible every day and completed two comprehensive Bible study courses offered by the Salvation Army. I continued to write poetry, sometimes writing three or four poems per day. It seemed like there was a fountain of words inside of me spewing out. Oftentimes, the poems were an expression of previous emotions suppressed years or decades earlier that were trapped inside of me. By writing the poems I was able to release those emotions. I was stuck in a terrible place but worst of all I was stuck with Danielle Lacost for my parole hearings. She gave me three 12 month defers in a row followed by a 24-month defer which was increased to a 36 month defer by an even more zealous parole chairman. I took them to court. It was beyond belief that I could go from an 8-month a few years earlier to a 36 month defer, essentially a pronouncement that I would never be paroled. I was sure that the state courts would find it arbitrary and capricious but what I didn't realize at the time was that the judges were also becoming more oppressive and less willing to grant any prisoner relief under any circumstances. Each time a prisoner would win something in state court other prisoners would take heart and file for relief as well. Judges learned not to rule in favor of any prisoner.

Several years after I was transferred to Stanley I felt the Holy Spirit speak to my heart telling me that I should draw. I've never been an artist. I was more of a stick figure kind of guy but I heeded the call. I bought drawing supplies and books on how to draw. I spent three to six hours every day drawing in the day room. I met Wilfredo who was a phenomenal artist who would sit and watch me doggedly plodding away on my drawings. He began to give me tips and advice and I soon got to where I would go as far as I could and then turn my drawings over to him. In 10 minutes, he would take my mediocre efforts and turn them into beautiful graphite artwork. He explained as he worked. I watched and listened and applied what he taught me on my next drawings. I donated some of my drawings to Safe Streets Art Foundation and they were so impressed with the quality of my work that they displayed my drawings in various art galleries in the Washington DC area. I gave away most of my drawings and sold a few. Meanwhile I was still submitting my poems for publication and occasionally getting paid for them. A wonderful thing happened through Safe Streets. A woman who was a prolific writer and author was looking for a prisoner pen pal and contacted them to ask for the name of somebody she could write. They gave her my name and she wrote me that first letter. From there blossomed the most wonderful caring relationship between myself and Katya Sabaroff Taylor. We exchanged poems, wrote simultaneous stories based on two-word titles that we picked together and did all kinds of wonderful things through the mail. It was great and so wonderful to have a positive reinforcing person in my life during that time.

While at Stanley I got an unexpected letter from Sue, the woman who I had been with when I first got sent to prison. She had lived her life, spent decades married and had a daughter. She was now divorced, living alone and decided to find out what happened to me. Little did she suspect that decades later I'd still be in prison. We started corresponding, then visiting. We spent many hours getting to know one another again. We each felt a need in the other and together we helped each other heal and grow. It was wonderful to once again have someone who cared about me in my life. Meanwhile Governor Scott Walker won reelection and the courts upheld the 36 month defer. I finally had to admit that it would never be possible to get relief through the courts and gave up litigating. I was devastated and had to face the reality that I probably would never get out of prison. In spite of this, I stayed true to my spiritual path and resolved to continue to do God's will in my life no matter what. God doesn't exist to make good things happen in your life – even though sometimes we get blessings. He is there to give you the strength to carry on in spite of the bad things that happen.

Indomitability

I caught the scent of clover
On the wind the other day,
Evoking memories of the idyllic
Wisconsin meadows of my youth.
It was a hopeful, nostalgic reminder
That better days will return despite
The endless imprisonment which grinds
And crushes me like glaciers level mountains.
It seems that all will be destroyed
In that slow, inexorable pulverization.
Yet just as the land healed itself after
Each glacial onslaught, so, too, I become
Whole and complete each time the
Prison oppression obliterates me.
My memories of wild flowers, nettles and
Monarch butterflies on milkweed cannot be
Stifled by concrete and steel or the
Wanton harshness of oppression, just as
My soul cannot be devoured by vindictive
Malice oozing from the sores of the correctional
Monster which has tried so hard to devour me
Yet finds me indigestible, wanting to spit me out
But too tenacious to let me go.
The clover which called to mind all that
I was and will be again is there to remind
Me once again that nothing is forever and
Today does not equal tomorrow.
In my heart and in my soul I am

Forever free, heedless of the shackles –
Both real and metaphorical – which keep
Me from the brighter future which is both
Birthright and destiny.
Let each day be another testament to an
Indomitable spirit, confidence born of
Survival in a time and place where
Insanity rules the roost, harshness is
Applauded and justice went out the
Window with yesterday's foul air.
September 4, 2017

One aspect of medium security in Stanley was the application of the 2-year rule. No prisoner could work for any department within the institution for more than 2 years. He then could not work for that same department again for at least 2 years. Because of the imposition of Truth In Sentencing, prisoners were now serving decades longer in prison - usually at the same prison without possibility of transfer. The only way to open up the higher-paying prison jobs was to terminate the current prisoner's job after 2 years. The administration claimed that it was to prevent fraternization between prisoners and staff. In my opinion, that's a bunch of baloney – especially in Stanley. There is no opportunity to fraternize. There are no secret places, nowhere that a prisoner and staff member could go to be alone and unobserved. As a result of the policy, I had to scramble for a new job every 2 years. After my 2 years in the library, I ended up working in the housing unit, first as a dining room worker and then as a personal laundry attendant. After a while I was able to get a job as a clerk in the chapel. I loved the job but once again I could only stay for 2 years and ended up working in the housing unit again until I was able to get back into the library. And so it went until I was given a new lease on life by Governor Tony Evers.

FREEDOM AT LAST

While I was serving another 24 month defer after the 36 month defer, Democrat Tony Evers won the gubernatorial election. He was backed by WISDOM, an organization committed to halving the prison population. He appointed a parole chairman to fulfill the mandate to release old law prisoners who had been kept in prison needlessly for decades. I tried to persuade the new chairman to reduce my current defer and transition me to release right away but he declined. I had to wait for my current 24 month defer to be served. He had gotten so many complaints and gotten so much opposition to Danielle Lacost and Steve Landreman - two parole commission members who had de facto control of the parole commission - that he decided to remove them from the commission. They didn't share his vision for releasing old law prisoners and eventually left to be replaced by commission members who viewed potential parolees based on facts rather than subjective ideology. I finally got a hearing before one of the new commission members and received an 11 month defer and endorsement to return to minimum security to prepare for release. Chairman John Tate II reviewed that decision and reduced it to 8 months.

I was transferred to Oak Hill shortly after that where I received a request from the parole commission for a pre-release investigation report. It was approved and I was slated to be picked up by Sue.

Getting Out of Prison

One guy ran all the way
From his housing unit to
The administration building where
His parents were waiting to
Take him home – for the fourth time –
After his dad drove to Michigan to
Buy him some pot to
Smoke during his homecoming.
Another guy, much older and
More sedate, told his friend to
Have a pack of cigarettes in the truck
When he picked him up so
He could go back to committing
Suicide by cigarette ASAP.
Each prisoner, regardless of
Time served, has his own
Fantasy about what makes for
A great homecoming.
In a few days, I'll
Slowly walk to the administration
Building savoring each moment,
Anticipating my release fantasy . . .
October 17, 2021

It was a surreal experience to walk out of the front gate after 37 years. I was afraid that something would happen at the last minute to derail my release. While in Stanley, I had lost my faith in having good outcomes in my life. I was happy and hopeful but unable to take it all in stride. As I finish this Memoir over 3 years after my release I am still scared. I'm afraid that's something unexpected is going to happen to thrust me back into the nightmare. I had so many plans for what I was going to do, what I was going to accomplish upon release. Most of my goals have not been reached. Somewhere along the way I lost whatever it was that made me capable of doing great things. I now have one goal: to never return to prison. As long as I accomplish that I'll declare my life as success and slowly fade into obscurity. I spent 37 years in prison for murder when no murder was committed. I stabbed a man of self-defense and was convicted of murder based on lies and jury instructions which denied me a fair trial. I will never be vindicated, I'll never get that 37 years of my life back and I'll never get reparations for the wrong done to me. On the other hand, I never would have been able to do the emotional healing I needed to do and reclaim my spiritual path without facing the horrendous adversity of my decades-long imprisonment and surviving it. Indeed, as the title of this book says, I came out better than I went in.

POSTSCRIPT

Based on the foregoing, you may think that my life is a drab, meaningless existence noteworthy only because I'm no longer in prison. Not at all. I have made a wonderful life for myself out in the free world. I met a wonderful woman whom I have been with for the last 3 years. We live in a beautiful home and have a motorcycle we use to travel hither and yon during the warm summer months.

The world is as you perceive it to be. I choose to perceive my world as a beautiful place full of wonderful adventures, good times, good friends and blessings raining down upon our heads like a summer shower. My heart overflows with love and gratitude for all the great people who have come into my life to enrich it in so many ways.

Getting from where I was to where I am now is another interesting story which will have to wait for another day to be told.

APPENDIX I: PHOTOS OF DRAWINGS

This appendix contains photos of some of the hundreds of drawings I made over the years. Many of them were random black and white photos from old books, most of which I no longer have access to and no longer know the name of the book or the original photographer. Several of them are of people I knew, such as my mother and Rick Gosling (since deceased).

Self Portrait

Photo by Dorthea Lang – Migrant Mother 1936

Photo by Don McCullen - Bangladesh 1971

Mennonite Couple, based on a photo in the book "Look In America" by the editors of Look Magazine (1948)

Lighthouse Eastern Seaboard

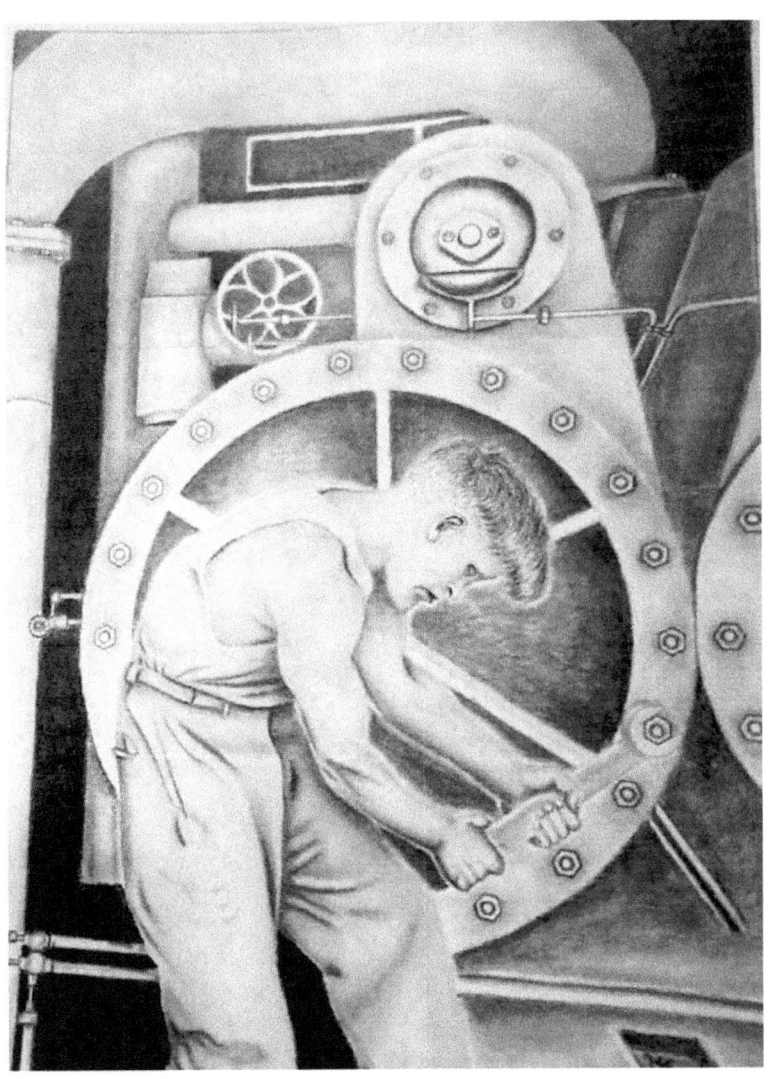

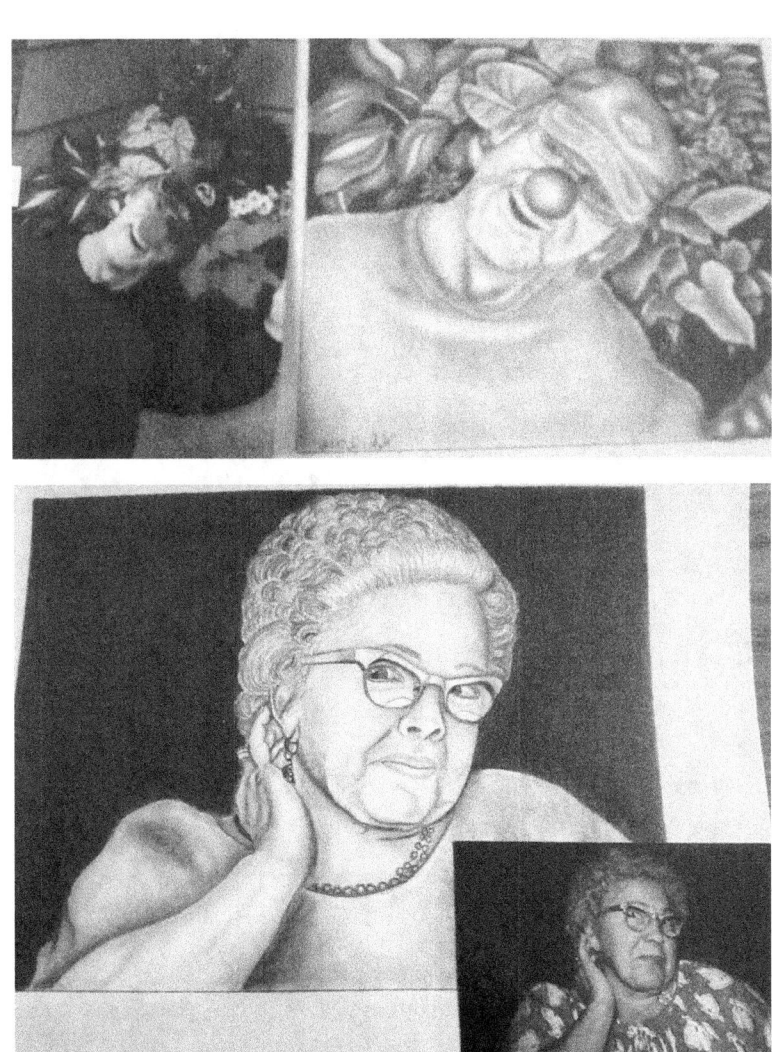

APPENDIX 2: TWENTY HARLANISMS TO LIVE BY

Table of Contents

INTRODUCTION

A spiritual path is a journey that lasts for as long as you exist. There is no final destination to reach where you can stop. There are many resting areas along the way. I have often found that I make progress in fits and starts. I will do a period of intense meditations and ritual-to reach a higher-state than ever before. I will then take the time to assimilate what I learned into my life and actions.

THE FUTURE IS WHAT YOU MAKE IT

Tony Robbins was very good at identifying and using gems of wisdom which were mined by others. One of his exercises was first propounded by Viktor Frankl, a man who survived the Nazi concentration camps. He said that the test for determining if you are living your life in the best manner possible is to think of yourself as a 75-year-old man or woman in your rocking chair looking back on your life. If you will be satisfied with what you did with your life when it is all over then you are doing the right thing. But if all you see when you look back are regrets and should-haves, then it is time to make a change.

That's what your future is all about. Taking the time now to make the plans and take the steps which will give you the future you will be able to look back upon at the end of your life with pride and satisfaction. To plan your future, you need to set goals and benchmarks by which to measure your progress.

Having written the foregoing before I reached my 70s, it seemed appropriate to use the age of 75 for looking back on one's life. But now that I am older, I realize that age is just a number. Your chronological age is not the determining factor. I prefer to view my life in terms of psychological age – how old you feel. Some people are done living in their 60s, others are vibrant and active past a century. The rocking chair test should occur when you feel that you've done all you're going to do and are ready to shuffle off this mortal coil. That age is different for each of us and it's up to you to decide when that time is for you.

SHOOT FOR THE STARS

The best way to build your future is to set definite goals and then create measurable steps which will define the amount of your progress toward these goals. Do some brainstorming. Decide what you want to achieve and then break that down into individual steps.

When I was at Fox Lake, I resolved to earn a bachelor's degree in business administration. I had expected to be able to do it using grants from the state and federal government. But the anti-prisoner hysteria in the 1990s caused the United States Congress to deprive prisoners of access to Pell Grants. So I had to find another way.

The university had year-long contracts which covered up to 18 credits. I calculated how many credits I needed to graduate, what order I had to take the courses in to meet prerequisite requirements and how many contracts it would take to earn a degree. Armed with this information I set about earning the money to pay for my first contract. I began working at Badger State Industries for $1.00 per hour and saved my money. I was able to pay for my next contract in this manner. I sought additional funding from private sources and found two foundations who would each pay for one contract. I also had to pay for books, postage (all courses were via correspondence) and supplies. I borrowed text books from the Wisconsin Interlibrary Loan-program when they were available, I bought used books and resold them when the course was completed. I bought new books when there was no other way to obtain the books, which I then resold.

I looked at each class to determine the amount of studying which was required and how long it would take to complete. I calculated the time it would take to complete all the exams and homework. I set up a schedule for each contract to ensure that I finished all the courses within the one-year time period of the contract.

By carefully planning all my steps and setting goals and benchmarks to meet, I earned a Bachelor of Science degree in business administration majoring in marketing. I graduated summa cum laude with a 3.95 Grade Point Average. Setting goals to meet gives you a purpose in life, something to apply your talents to achieving. Life can be lived on auto-pilot where you get through each day only to face the next one with no thought to the future. Or, you can decide where you want to be in your life and set goals to get there. Do you really want to work all day at a dead-end job and come home to a few hours of mindless television before you go to bed only to do it all again the next day? I think not. Every day in your life is a choice. You can choose to have goals in your life and you can choose what goals to have. If you don't like the ones you currently have, set new ones. You are the boss of what direction your life takes. Make it a direction that fulfills you.

MEDITATION AND PRAYER

Everyone should apply effort toward enlightenment. Meditation is a good first step.

As is prayer and what is called Karma Yoga.

Meditation is as simple as sitting still and watching your breath as it flows in and out. Or it can involve complex visualizations, postures or breathing regimens. There are so many variations and possibilities out there that I can't tell you which ones to try. Each of us must find the practices which best suit us and use self-discipline to master them until we get results.

I can tell you generally what I have done. I used to regularly sit quietly in a chair with my spine straight, hands on my thighs. I let my breathing do what it wants while I observe it. Soon, the mind quiets down and profound epiphanies slowly bubble to the surface. I've had some great realizations through meditating but mostly the effects of meditation are more subtle. It helps me become calmer, more stable and tolerant. I also breathe through my heart chakra, a method of staying centered in a state of lovingkindness. When I view the world while in a state of compassion and empathy, I can feel love for all living beings.

In the past, I've done an assortment of practices. I have prayed, performed rituals and ceremonies, mastered different forms of Magick, engaged in exercises to control my mind, energized my chakras and performed pranayama (breathing exercises).

Bo Lozoff, best known as author of We're All Doing Time, tells a story in his book, Deep and Simple, about his conversation with a spiritual teacher who stated that nobody knew if or when enlightenment would come to them: "They are spontaneous moments of grace. They are accidents." Bo asked, "What is the point of doing intense spiritual practices if religious experiences are just accidents?" The sage replied, "To be as accident prone as possible." Far be it from me to contradict an enlightened spiritual teacher but I beg to differ. You may not achieve complete transformation but any person who pours his heart and soul into following a spiritual path with total commitment and dedication will achieve results. My first major breakthrough came when I did a six-month long regimen of invoking my Holy Guardian Angel using a complex ritual performed on the astral plane up to 4 times per day. If you want to transcend your ego badly enough, you will succeed.

I have also read about studies done by Professor Richard Davidson at the University of Wisconsin, Madison, involving Buddhist monks who have spent thousands of hours in meditation. By connecting numerous electrodes to their skulls, it has been possible to document the changes which have occurred in the activity in their brains. It was found that these monks had increased gamma waves, not only when they were meditating, but in between sessions as well. MRI scans also showed increased activity in the "right insula and caudate", areas of the brain associated with empathy and maternal love. Clearly, even if you do not achieve Samadhi in your meditation, you will at least make permanent, positive changes in yourself.

Prayer differs from meditation in that it is more of a beseeching a higher entity to interact with you in one way or another. Most often, prayer is for guidance, support or adoration. Years ago, I scorned prayer as something for those too weak-willed to forge their own path in life. But when Christ called me as one of His own in 2010, things changed. I switched over to prayer and realized that prayer is just as powerful as ritual or meditation. It is merely a different way to get to the same place. I pray for guidance often. I made so many bad choices in my life, I know that I need the Holy Spirit's input to guide me in the right direction. I also use prayer to count my blessings and thank the Holy Spirit for all the good things in my life. It requires surrendering to God's Will in your life. If you don't believe in God or reject that there is a divine force in the universe, that's up to you. I'm sharing what works for me and we each have to find our own path forward.

CORE TRANSFORMATION

I don't really understand the makeup of the human psyche. I'm like a car mechanic who can't explain the theory behind how everything works but when you bring your car to him, he can fix it.

Core transformation is sort of like hypnosis. It works for those who are receptive to it. Many people cannot open themselves up enough to be hypnotized. I would guess that it is the same thing that prevents some people from using core transformation effectively. I have had great results from the sessions I completed. I attribute this in part to all of the meditation I have done over the years and my desire to achieve results at any cost. It is a process of tapping into the subconscious to find out what is blocking us from being or doing what we want. I liken it to a short cut to enlightenment. Under the right conditions you can achieve in an hour what it would take years of conventional spiritual practices or psychotherapy to achieve.

The process has several other names. It was first called neuro-linguistic programming (NLP) by its creators. Tony Robbins adopted it and modified it slightly calling it neuro-associative conditioning (NAC). Connirae and Tamara Andreas also used the process. They wrote a very good do-it-yourself book called Core Transformation which I used to put myself through the process without assistance. The process is not for everybody. But it may be for you. Look into it and see if you can supercharge your spiritual path with this short cut to Nirvana (or at the very least, accomplish emotional healing so that you can let go of past trauma).

CHANGES – A BETTER WAY TO VIEW OTHER PEOPLE

There is good in everybody. Sometimes you gotta dig pretty deep to find it. But it's there. I used to believe that most people were a waste of good oxygen, that the world would be better off without them. Now I know better. It's all a matter of perception. If you perceive others as useless pieces of human excrement that's what they'll be. But if you approach others with the belief that there is good in every person you meet, it will show itself.

I first learned this when I lived and worked with other prisoners whom I couldn't stand to be around. I got tired of being upset and seething. I decided that there must be a better way. I had read somewhere or other that we are all divine spirits encased in physical bodies. If so, then even in those seemingly useless people I hated there had to be a divine essence just like me. I began to look beyond their words and actions to see what their mothers saw in them. As I looked deeper, I began to see what was good about them.

We are all works in process. We steadily grow and change. Not everyone is at the same level or grows at the same rate. Some try to better themselves. Others have betterment thrust upon them through life's circumstances. And a few are just treading water.

As I began to see others as luminous beings, I started being more accepting of them. I no longer seethed over actions of others. I didn't get angry. As I became more accepting of others, I began to act differently toward them. No longer did I walk around with barely concealed contempt for everybody. I had empathy for others. There was a surprising result which I never expected. As I began to regard others with good will in my heart, they seemed to feel it and respond to it as well. People were nicer to me regardless of whether I knew them or not. When I took the Get the Edge program at Oakhill, I received an aid to help me in this process.

Tony Robbins developed the theory that there are 5 basic human needs which drive people 's behavior (or maybe he just borrowed it from someone else). When I began looking past the actions of others to see what basic human need was motivating their behavior, I could better understand and relate to the other person. A person first needs security; after that comes variety; next is community; then a chance to contribute; and finally, a chance for self-improvement.

Everything each of us does can be traced to one of these 5 needs. When I faced an angry or threatening person, I could see he had not met his need for security yet. A person who is out trying every new thing that comes along is seeking to satisfy the need for variety. And so it goes for each of the basic human needs.

PERCEPTION: WHAT YOU SEE IS WHAT YOU GET

The world is as you perceive it to be. If you think the world is a terrible place full of lying, conniving selfish people, that is what you will find on your path through life. There is a fancy term for this called your reticular activating system. We, as people, notice what we are focused on. If you buy a new car, suddenly you see the same make and model everywhere you go. They were always there, you just never noticed them before.

Your basic personality is keyed to perceive those things which reinforce its philosophy on life. Those who think everything is determined by luck do not see the consequences of their actions. Whatever happens, good or bad, is caused by luck or fate. I used to believe this way. It was my perception of the world which left me to do as I pleased but unable to affect the outcome of my life. When I had the Vision of Cause and Effect, my worldview changed. I no longer perceive things as happening in my life based on luck or chance but rather as a result of the choices I make. I now perceive a world where results are obtained by conscientious application of effort to accomplish specific tasks which will achieve desired goals.

I now choose to perceive the world as a wonderful place full of good, caring people where I can make a positive difference in their lives by my actions. And as I perceive it, it has become the reality for me. The point is that if you don't like the life you are living and are currently unable to change the external circumstances of that life, you can always change how you choose to perceive it. Our perception is a prism which distorts the events of our lives in a manner which will match our beliefs. Those who view the world as a place of luck and fate, see events much differently than a person who thinks that one's actions will determine his or her future. That is why how you choose to perceive your life is so important.

CHOICES: TO CHOOSE OR NOT TO CHOOSE

Everything is a choice. Either a choice you make or refuse to make. Doing nothing, after all, is an equally valid choice. You can choose to relate to others in a positive, loving way or you can choose to spread venom and hatred throughout your life. I have met so many people in prison who are angry and bitter. They are unhappy and depressed. When I ask why, there is always some external cause or reason they blame it on. That is not really why they are unhappy. It is a matter of choice.

Each of us has the power to choose what we are going to feel like at any given moment. We can choose to be happy or not. When we blame external events for our negative states we are surrendering our power over ourselves and giving it to another. One guy told me that he could not celebrate Christmas because he was in prison. I told him he was choosing not to enjoy Christmas. He insisted that it was only Christmas if he was free and with his family. He failed to realize that he chose to be unhappy because he was in prison. Granted, prison is not a pleasant place. But that does not mean you are destined to suffer just because you are there. You can choose to focus on positive things and feel joy from them. Christmas is a state of mind and feeling which you can have at any time simply by choosing it over every other possible state. So it goes with your whole life. Everything is a choice because you control your own true reality.

TRUE REALITY: THE MATERIAL WORLD IS A MIRAGE THAT MATTERS

The material plane in which our bodies exist and function is the playground where we get experiences which allow our true natures to grow and evolve. The true reality where it really counts is inside each of us. It is no easy feat to find this reality. Often, it takes many hours of meditation and other spiritual practices to learn to get in touch with that reality. Mystics and sages of the past have often spoke of this, stating ,"All is illusion." But that term never really explains it. It is left for the seeker of truth to find it out for himself. It is an epiphany which comes to everyone who devotes himself to a spiritual path. A good parallel is trying to explain an orgasm to someone who has never had one. Sure, you can go into detail about how it feels. But until that first orgasm is experienced, words are inadequate to the task. It is something each of us must experience in order to know it.

Even the scientists of this age have come to concede that things which are seen by people as the solid material plane are in fact fields of energy. Quantum physics is a mind- boggling look at seemingly solid objects at their most basic level. It turns out that everything we once thought of as solid is in reality based on energy. I'll leave it to others to explain quantum physics as I am no expert on the subject. I can tell you that once you study the subject it will be much easier to accept that the True Reality is not the material plane.

The spiritual plane, upon which each of us exists, is accessible by turning your focus within and silencing the mind until it reveals itself to you. Once you gain an awareness of this reality you will realize that what goes on outside of you is only important in regard to how it helps you grow and evolve. I suppose skeptics will say that if you get hit by a truck or shot in the head you are dead regardless of your internal reality. The material world still matters but it is not the be-all and end-all that most people think it is. Your body may die but your spirit lives on in that True Reality and is able to harvest the effects of the incident which caused your death and benefit from it.

You don't need to take my word for this. Do your own meditations, follow your own spiritual path and find your own true reality. It is there waiting for you to develop the ability to perceive it.

THE EGO: GET OVER YOURSELF

There was a guy I met at Gordon who was a very charismatic and likeable fellow. He was a unique person who generally stood head and shoulders above everyone else in every way. He had one major failing. Because of his awareness of his own abilities in comparison with everyone else he had an overinflated sense of self-importance. I used to tell him: "It's not always all about you." I said it so often that it became a standing joke between us. It did help him become more aware of his self-centeredness and he did make an effort to be more considerate of others. He was not perfect - none of us are. He was a crackhead who lost control of his life and ended up in prison. Even with all his good qualities he was still just another person with strengths and weaknesses.

I was also at one time an arrogant, pompous ass. I was a renowned jailhouse lawyer and had much knowledge and education compared to other guys I encountered. In my eyes, it made me special and better than everyone else. I looked down on others and treated them with distain. When I first learned that I didn't know everything worth knowing and began my journey of self-discovery, I had to reevaluate my opinion of myself. I joined

Self-help Group at Fox Lake. At each meeting we would get into small groups and discuss some lesson or situation provided by the group. It involved each of us expressing ourselves. I took the time to listen to others. Suddenly, I was hearing great insights and wisdom from people I had previously dismissed as beneath me. I had to learn to not judge others. So many times since then I have been blessed with gems of wisdom from the most unlikely people. It made me realize that I am no better than anyone else. Each of us are unique individuals with our own assets and liabilities. It is our uniqueness which makes us valuable.

That was my first step in coming to grips with my ego. The second step occurred when I was at Kettle Moraine and died to who I was. My body lived on but my ego died. It was no longer what I wanted that mattered, it was doing God's will to the best of my understanding and ability. It requires a selflessness, a willingness to put one's personal wants and desires behind the greater good. I gave up my ego because I no longer wanted to live just to satisfy my personal desires. The pain of living was greater than any satisfaction of my desires could compensate for. I have to live to serve a greater purpose.

My ego is not dead. It is still a part of me. It is no longer in control. I still try to better myself. I still save money, make plans for the future, seek comfort for myself and want what's best for Harlan. But I constantly remind myself that I am not my ego. It is merely a means to gain experience in the world which can help me grow and develop as a person. Many paths of spiritual attainment teach that the ego must be totally destroyed - annihilated - as one proceeds along the path. But I am not sure that is necessary. I think it is only necessary that one's choices in life are based on fulfilling a greater purpose rather than on sating the ego's desires. Maybe I'm just not far along enough on my spiritual path to see Truth yet or maybe my ego is blinding me to what yet needs to be done. I am in a committed relationship with a wonderful woman and I learned that the best relationships are when both partners put the wants and the needs of their partner first. When you love someone unselfishly, their wants and needs become more important than your own. If only one partner feels this way, it's an unbalanced relationship. If neither partner feels this way, it's a dysfunctional relationship.

What is my greater purpose? I'm not sure. Perhaps to help others find their spiritual paths. This book may be a part of that greater purpose. I have a feeling that there is something in my future which I must do - my greater purpose - and all my efforts at this point in time are to prepare myself so I am ready when the time comes. Time will tell...

You don't need to go live in a cave. You don't need to punish yourself through self-denial and privation. Asceticism may be fine for those who choose it, but it is not necessary. You can live well, enjoy creature comforts and take care of your own needs. The point is not to let self-indulgence become the purpose of your existence. Live for the Greater Purpose.

MITAKAYU OASIN

This is a Sioux phrase which means "all my relations." It is one of the hardest spiritual lessons for me to experience. It essentially means that we are all related to each other and everything else. It is only the ego which makes us feel like we are individual, separate and cut off from others. I know all this intellectually but I have a hard time feeling it.

The method of a spiritual path is to come to a deep knowing that something is true by experiencing it. In all the other areas I have written about I have come to the truth through direct personal experience. This experience still eludes me in its totality. It is easier for me to feel a oneness with nature than with many other human beings. A beautiful sunset, a bright sunny day, an eagle as it soars across the sky all touch my soul and I can feel it is a part of me. Yet I need to do more. And I will. My seeking will continue for as long as I live.

FORGIVENESS

"To err is human, to forgive is divine." That is a famous quote by Alexander Pope in his poem, <u>An Essay on Criticism,</u> and I guess there is some truth in it. We all make mistakes and many of us hate to admit it when we do. For me, forgiving somebody else's mistakes is much harder than admitting my own. As I've said before, I hold grudges. At least I used to. Not so much any more. I learned the divine art of forgiveness.

In the mid-1990s, while I was in Fox Lake and just beginning on my path of transformation, I received a letter from a guy confessing to having turned me in to the police years earlier. I ended up getting arrested on drug charges and messed up years of my life. I already knew he ratted on me and had him on my list of things to do. I had patience. I didn't mind waiting a couple of decades to get even. The life sentence I received got in the way of more immediate retribution but it by no means meant that I would not still have my vengeance. With my new mindset where I was questioning all my old values and seeking a better way to live, I had to reevaluate my get-even commitment. Why was it so important to pay this guy back for what he did to me? What could possibly be gained by it? I was the one selling drugs in the first place. Had I not sold drugs he could not have set me up with an undercover agent so it appeared that I was at least partly responsible for what happened to me. Now that was an unpleasant thought. That I had to blame myself instead of someone else for what went wrong in my life.

Reluctantly, I came to the conclusion that I ought to forgive him and put it all behind me.

I wrote him back a short note which read something like this: "I already knew you snitched on me and I forgive you. Go forth and live your life in peace and happiness." A burden was lifted from me. It felt funny but good at the same time. We corresponded for a while after that. I learned that he had been living on the West Coast and became a meth addict. He did so much meth he began having constant hallucinations that demons were after him. He believed that I sent the demons after him and contacted me so I would call off the demons. I sent him some rituals to use for self-defense and never heard from him again.

This experience taught me not to hold grudges, to cut other people some slack and to accept them as they are. It allowed me to look back on other aspects of my life and forgive there as well. I forgave my brother for all the misery he inflicted on me while he was alive. And I forgave me for taking his life. He was wrong for what he did to me but I was also wrong for taking his life. At the time, I could see no other way to be free of his tyranny. Maybe there wasn't. Maybe that was the way I chose because it was the easy way out.

Each time I reached out and forgave someone whom I had been holding a grudge against I felt a burden lift from me. I freed up energy that I had invested in that grudge to use for more positive things. I felt lighter and freer. I'm still a work in progress. I must be constantly vigilant that I do not hold perceived wrongs against other people. I do an emotional inventory on a regular basis to make sure no new grudges are lodging themselves in my psyche. When I do find a sore spot, I make sure I also find a way to let it go and forgive whomever is involved. It ain't easy, but it's rewarding.

FITNESS: FIND YOUR OWN LEVEL

Do I even have any business expounding on fitness? Perhaps. Maybe my story can give others the motivation to find their own level of fitness.

When I was a toddler, I was always sickly and skinny. I had a severe coordination problem. I would try to run and trip over my own two feet and skin my knees. I skinned my knees so many times they became infected and I had to go to the hospital to get rid of the infection. My father thought I was doing it on purpose so he started calling me "Stumblebum" to get me to quit it. What an enlightened form of treatment that was! When I started kindergarten the teachers noticed my problem, gave me a series of exercises to do and corrected the coordination deficiency. However, I began overeating after I started school and became obesely fat. My parent's philosophy on nutrition was to let their kids eat as much as they wanted of whatever they wanted so I stayed fat until I was 12 years old. Then I put myself on my own diet to lose weight. I pretty much starved myself until most of the fat was gone and kept it off from then on.

I never exercised regularly, never ate properly and never took care of myself. As an adult, I drank as much alcohol as I wanted.

I did not have to worry about weight loss or gain. When I had a motorcycle accident at age 18 where I crushed my leg, I lost weight from not eating and having staph infection. I dipped down to 130 pounds. I eventually gained the weight back and stayed pretty much at 150 pounds. I worked at a foundry for a while and my weight went up to about 165 pounds from the extra muscle I gained from the hard work. Then it went back down to 150.

Facing a life sentence made me decide to exercise and eat right so I would have many years of health after I got out of prison if I ended up serving a life sentence. I began to jog and lift weights and cut back on my food intake. At one point, I dropped down to 138 pounds but I was too skinny. My weight eventually stabilized at around 150 again. I didn't believe in supplements. I believed my body should take whatever I put into it and thrive on it.

When I was at Fox Lake, a guy gave me some Unilivers - desiccated liver tablets. I started taking two a day just because I had them, not because I expected anything from them. But a funny thing happened to me. From the time of my motorcycle accident, I had always had low energy. I was easily exhausted. When I went to the gym to work out, I usually had to take a nap afterward because I was so tired. Suddenly, I found myself lifting 30% more weight, doing more repetitions in each set and not having to take a nap after each workout. I couldn't figure out what was going on. It never occurred to me to connect taking the pills with my increased strength. As the phenomenon continued it finally dawned on me that the changes occurred a couple of weeks after I started taking the Unilivers. It was the only thing which had changed in my life so it had to be the pills which changed everything.

I became a believer in supplements after that. I started ordering Unilivers, protein powder, vitamins - everything that the canteen sold. I monitored my protein intake, cut down on junk food and empty calories. My weight went up to 167 pounds while I was taking creatine and then dropped back down to stabilize at 160 pounds after I stopped taking it.

Recently, a guy asked me to help him lose weight and get into shape. I have seen many guys claim to want to get into shape but who aren't willing to make the sacrifices it takes to reach their goals. But I agreed to be his trainer and guided him on what exercises to do and what to eat.

He started out at 230 pounds and slowly dropped the weight. In just under 3 months; he lost 20 pounds. He has more muscle mass and less fat. He is due to be released in a few months and wanted to be under 200 pounds by his release date. I wasn't an easy taskmaster. It is hard work to lose weight, much harder than not putting it on in the first place. It is especially hard to lose weight in a healthy way so that you drop the fat and keep the muscle mass. The hardest thing to accept is that by eating the right foods at the right time you can lose more weight than by just starving yourself.

The point is you will look better, feel better, live longer and have a better quality of life by getting fit and staying that way.

EXCUSES: EVERYBODY HAS ONE – OR TWENTY

You know the old saying: Excuses are like assholes, every-body has one. Excuses are how we justify not doing what we know we need to do. The first step is learning the difference between a good reason and an excuse.

If you have a good reason, something that a disinterested person would agree with, then you can shirk your commitment or responsibility with a clear conscience. Often, we don't feel like doing something and dredge up some pretext for not doing it. That's an excuse and is unacceptable on a spiritual path. When I was in Waupun, I was moved from a single cell to a double cell as a form of punishment when I was causing the prison administration problems. At the time, I was unable to meditate with someone else in close proximity to me. I complained and filed a lawsuit which I fought for years and eventually lost. I started out refusing to do any meditating because "they" made it impossible for me to do so. It wasn't my fault, it was theirs. My stubborn streak kicked in and I resolved not to do anything until I could do it on my terms. But the more I thought about it, I came to realize that not getting my way was an excuse I was using to prevent me from doing what I really wanted and needed to do. I could spend my time fighting over my right to practice my religious beliefs or I could follow my path to the best of my ability under the restrictions placed upon me. I chose the latter and learned the difference between a reason and an excuse. I didn't make much progress at the time but it set the stage for what was to come later.

I'm sure you see the point. Don't let excuses stop you from being and doing what is important to you in life. If it wasn't difficult, it wouldn't be worth doing.

SELF-DISCIPLINE: WHERE IT ALL BEGINS

This is one tough character trait to develop if you don't already have it. It is so necessary for most of us if we want to accomplish anything in our lives and so hard to acquire.

Sure, there are those for whom the challenges in life come easy. They sail through life effortlessly. Everything they want in life seems to fall into their laps. For the rest of us mere mortals it takes sweat, blood and pain to get anywhere.

I've always been strong-willed. Others would probably call me stubborn or mule-headed. I get a bug up my ass about something or other and my mind locks. I'll be damned if I back down, quit or give up. I have been able to turn this stubborn streak into an asset by using it to achieve self-discipline. Recently, one guy started calling me "Mr. Relentless" because I stayed committed to my decision to become an accomplished artist. I went from essentially zero talent to a graphite artist who had his works displayed in various art galleries.

It isn't easy to make yourself do what is difficult, distasteful or unpleasant. I first used self-discipline in the 6th grade when

I was fat and starved myself for months to lose weight. I had such terrible hunger pangs. I yearned to eat but I decided that I wanted to be slimmer and made the sacrifices necessary to reach that goal.

I also went for 37 years in prison without one misconduct report in my record, a feat unparalleled by any other prisoner in Wisconsin as far as I know. It took lots of self-control and discipline to endure decades of petty, arbitrary rules and harassment without once getting a conduct report placed on my record.

I suppose self-discipline could be called self-denial or self-restriction because it constitutes stopping yourself from doing what you want to do in order to do what's best for you.

For those of us who meditate regularly or start a fitness routine, self-discipline is what we need to make us get up at 4:00 a.m. to assume our asana or go to the gym. Our selfish selves (our egos) may be crying out to sleep a little later but our disciplined selves make us get up and do what we know needs doing.

The point is that you need to learn to master your urges or desires, to subjugate the cravings of your lower nature. That takes self-discipline and the more you use it, the stronger it gets.

I FEEL GREAT AND SO SHOULD YOU

Pat Croce wrote a book called <u>I Feel Great</u>. His premise is that if you make it a point to say you feel great regularly it becomes a self-fulfilling prophecy. On the other hand, if you answer the question of "How are you?" by saying "okay", "not bad", "getting by" or any other less than positive affirmation it will also become a self-fulfilling prophecy. He had a lot more wisdom in his book but that was the concept that had the most impact on me.

I'm sort of a bipolar kind of guy although I have never been formally diagnosed as such.

I prefer to think of it as manic/depressive since that seems to describe it more accurately.

I used to wonder how I could go from absolutely ecstatic to suicidally depressed in the blink of an eye. It was while I was in Waupun that I first noticed this phenomenon. I did so many drugs and drank so much before coming to prison that I never noticed any mood changes. I was always too high or drunk or hung over to pay any attention. When I realized that I was manic/ depressive I concluded that I would no longer be that way. If I

219

had to be one or the other then I would choose to be manic all the time. Strangely enough, it worked most of the time. I read "I Feel Great" while I was at Oakhill and since it advised me to do what I had more or less been doing for years anyway, I took to it like a duck to water. Even on those days when I felt less-than-stellar I forced myself to always respond when asked how I am to say: "I feel great!" The more I said it, the better I felt.

The "Get the Edge" program gave me a chance to expand on this theme. Tony Robbins spoke in his book, <u>Awaken the Giant Within</u>, of using more words to describe emotional states and thereby allow yourself to experience a greater range of emotions. I started thinking of other superlatives to describe how I felt. My current favorite is FANTASTIC but I also like fabulous, extraordinary, blessed and awesome.

The point is that how you feel every day is a choice and when you choose to feel great every day you will find that it comes easier to you the more you repeat the affirmation.

AN OPEN MIND IS A DOORWAY TO OPPORTUNITY

Have you ever met a person who thinks they know it all and won't listen to anyone else on any subject? I used to be one of those. You couldn't tell me anything. What a difference there is when you step out of your ego and look at life from a new perspective. You may be right, you may be wrong. You are no longer afraid to see the other side of the coin. No progress can be made on a spiritual path until you let go of your emotional investment in your beliefs and let the Holy Spirit show you the truth.

I used to have to be right all the time. I could not accept the possibility that I was wrong in anything. If you didn't agree with me, it was because something was wrong with you and you needed help. Mostly, I would keep to myself and look down on others with disdain and scorn.

Now it is a new day and a new attitude. I constantly search out others who may have the knowledge or wisdom I have not yet encountered. Where would I be now if I had not opened up my mind long enough to listen to the instructor in the anger management group? It was a paradigm-shifting experience.

What if there is another such experience waiting for me out there somewhere right now which I might miss if I don't take the time to listen, to know and to understand? My path to God is too important to me to risk missing that next experience simply because I was too obstinate to drink when offered the Elixir of Life.

I like to use the phrase, "You don't know what you don't know until you know it." There are many things I didn't know existed that would have benefited me over the years. I'm always searching for that next nugget of wisdom that hasn't been mined in my life yet. When I find it, I make it a part of who I am going forward.

GIVING A LITTLE OR GIVING A LOT

Melita Denning and Osbourne Phillips wrote a series of books back in the 1970s detailing their particular path to enlightenment and I always remember one thing they said about material possessions (including money): Give all you can, get all you can.

Some authors have argued that in today's economic system there is unlimited wealth. Therefore, everyone may freely acquire and hoard as much as they want without an adverse effect on society or others. I don't quite agree with this. I believe there is a finite amount of wealth and resources available to the human race at any given time. It may be a very large amount but it is still limited.

I see nothing wrong with gathering enough material goods to allow you to live comfortably and securely all of your life while taking care of your dependents and other financial obligations. But after the first few million, what possible use for, or justification for, amassing further wealth can you give? There are quite a few billionaires who started with nothing and got all of their wealth in one lifetime. Those are amazing people who did something extraordinary. Yet I feel they must be flawed in some way. What reason do you give yourself for pouring your heart and soul into acquiring that second billion? Wouldn't you be better off to turn your efforts elsewhere at some point?

Bill Gates, founder of Microsoft, is one of those who amassed an excessive amount of wealth and I am gratified to see him intent on pouring so much of it into programs to aid less fortunate people. A billionaire can have a greater impact than a pauper simply because he has the means at his disposal to do so. This principle applies to all people at all levels of wealth. Give all you can, get all you can. When you reach your comfort level, try giving of yourself to others instead of wasting your vitality collecting excess wealth. And on your way up to your comfort level, share a little along the way with those less fortunate. Buddhists say that doing good deeds has merit. Try to put a little of that into your life and see if you can make a difference.

LOVE

No self-respecting book on finding a spiritual path would be complete without a discourse on love. There is romantic love and then there is selfless love. I learned about and experienced romantic love from my second wife whom I married while I was in Fox Lake. I remember the day I fell in love with her. She came to visit me and I was smitten. I resolved to win her love and began writing her long love letters pouring my heart out to her. It was such an extraordinary experience for me. I never opened myself up to anyone before. I am grateful to her for the many things I learned by giving myself to her so completely. Unfortunately, we grew apart and finally separated years later. At the time we came together we were in sync. Later, we grew in different directions and it became clear we were on different paths. I am sorry for all the pain our separation caused her but I believe she would have suffered worse had we stayed together longer.

I learned about selfless love after I gave my life to God. I was at Oakhill taking the Get the Edge course when Cay started asking us to define what somebody had to do to make us feel loved. I started reeling off a shopping list of have-tos: have to come to visit me, have to write to me, have to accept my collect calls, have to run errands for me, etc. She said it's no wonder I didn't feel loved if all those conditions had to be met in order for me to feel loved. After the class, I thought about it and concluded that she was right. I could feel loved any time I wanted if I changed what it meant for me to feel loved. I feel loved every time I give love. My emotional state is no longer dependent on someone else's actions. It is up to me to decide when and how I feel loved.

Now I make an effort to love everyone I meet regardless of whether they meet my personal, ego-driven criteria or not. The more I love others, the more loved I feel. About a year after I was released from prison, I was blessed with a wonderful partner whom I currently live with. I feel that the secret to a lasting, loving relationship is if each person puts their partner ahead of themselves. But whether you have a romantic love or not, you can always be filled with the Greater Love which comes from God, exists in all of us and extends to all people.

GRATITUDE IS A DAILY EXERCISE

I am so grateful for all the wonderful things in my life. I am grateful for my daughter and grandchildren and for all my other relatives. I haven't seen many of them for decades but I am grateful I have them in my heart. I often take a gratitude inventory. I count all my blessings on a regular basis. I am blessed with intelligence, health, fitness and so many other things I can't count them all. There are so many less-fortunate people in the world than I. My heart goes out to them and I pray that God will pour his blessings out on them as well. I didn't always feel this way. I used to focus on what I didn't have that others had and which I wanted. I wanted their good looks, good luck, money, abilities, possessions. I wanted so many other things others had it's no wonder that I was always dissatisfied. The Ten Commandments in the Bible speaks about not coveting your neighbor's goods, wife, etc. Being envious of others is a sure path to dissatisfaction. I'm not saying that people should not go out and try to better themselves or acquire the things they want. You should set goals and work toward them with all your might. The point is that if you take time to sit back and appreciate everything you already have, your life will become more fulfilling, you will be happier and you may find that you already possess what you thought you were seeking.

Gratitude for the good things in your life is the easy part. Can you also learn to be grateful for the painful lessons in your life? I crushed my leg in a motorcycle accident when I was 18 years old. I had years of pain and suffering before my leg healed. I ended up crippled for life. Now, as I age, my ankle is deteriorating. I suffer pain day in and day out. Yet I can look back on my accident and admit that I needed that lesson in my life to help me grow as a person. Before I was crippled, I believed solely in physical prowess. Might makes right. Only the strongest survive. When my strength and stamina were broken by the accident, I had to learn to live another way. I could no longer just beat people up to get what I wanted. I had to learn to interact with others. I eventually went to college and earned a degree. Now I am known for erudition rather than violence. I hated all the physical suffering my injury caused me (and still does) but I am grateful for the lesson I learned which allowed me to move on to the next stage of my life.

GOD'S WILL

I believe each of us is here to do God's Will in our life. God has a purpose for each of us, that for which we were born. For some, it seems that they grow up knowing what they want to do, how they want to do it and when they should do it. I, for one, have spent most of my life wandering aimlessly without a clue about why I'm even here as a living, breathing human being. I am sure many of the readers of this book feel the same way. There must be more to life than making money, buying the latest high-tech gadget or experiencing the newest rides at Great America. The challenge is to find that purpose and fulfill it. It is there but sometimes you gotta search for it. The longer and harder the search, the greater the reward when you finally find God's Will in your life. Do not settle for mediocrity. Find what you are here to accomplish and strive for it with all your might.

Bo Lozoff, a person for whom I have a lot of respect, speaks of two necessary aspects which should be in every person's life: communion and community. Communion is doing the spiritual practices which will help you get in touch with the Holy Spirit. It may be prayer, mantras, yoga or any other means of which there are many. This connection provides the strength, energy and inspiration to carry on in your daily life in a meaningful manner. Community is your connection to others. As we gain from our spiritual connection, we should reach out to others to give of ourselves. One person's spiritual journey, as joyful and profound as it may be, is only a small part of humanity's spiritual journey. Reach out to help others to realize their potential as well. You may have the opportunity to lead another to his or her spiritual path or you may simply help a homeless person find a place to live. Whatever it is and how it fits into your life is up to you to decide. But it should be there as part of who you are as a person.

Now you know as much as I do, probably more. May God bless you and keep you safe from hurt and from harm and from evil.

www.ingramcontent.com/pod-product-compliance
Lightning Source LLC
Chambersburg PA
CBHW070912130626
46555CB00001B/94